SAFETY SENSE AT PLAY

BY

HEWARD GRAFFTEY

SAFETY SENSE AT PLAY

BY

HEWARD GRAFFTEY

Safety Sense Enterprises, Inc.
Ottawa, Ontario, Canada

SAFETY SENSE AT PLAY
by Heward Grafftey

Copyright © 1991
Registration No.: 410396

First Edition. All rights reserved.
No part of this book may be reproduced, stored in a retrieval system, or transmitted in any form or by any means electronic, mechanical photocopying, recording, or otherwise without the written permission of the publisher.

Cover Design: Karen Rasmussen
Inside Artwork: Karen Rasmussen
Edited by Dennis Bockus, The Editorial Centre
Managing Consultant: Suzanne Sarda, ABMS, Ottawa, Canada

Safety Sense Enterprises, Inc.
P.O. Box 9512, Station T
Ottawa, Ontario   K1G 3V2
(613) 830-9342 FAX: (613) 830-4284

ISBN: 0-9695-568-0-2

Édition française: SÉCURITÉ EN TÊTE AU JEU
ISBN: 0-9695-568-1-0

DEDICATION

This book is dedicated to the memory of the following people known to me who lost their lives in recreational or sporting activities accidents: Don Brown, Fred Fyles, Aird Nesbeitt, Michel Mireault, Geoff Taylor, Frank Carr, and John Dohan.

TABLE OF CONTENTS

INTRODUCTION

Many people who engage in sport recreational activities do so neither well nor wisely. To enjoy play activities one has to be free from injury and illness. Yet injury in sport and recreational activities is primarily a result of accidents.

Consider that about five percent of all emergency-room-treated injuries to children aged one through four years involve playground equipment; that the overall injury rate for children participating in recreational, community, or school sports is between three and 11 percent, and that about 18 percent of all off-duty injuries to workers occur while they are pursuing a sport or recreational activity.

Safety Sense Enterprises believes that sport and recreational injuries can be reduced through the use of adequate equipment controls, along with effective sport safety leadership, which would provide safe play areas, proper equipment and facilities, adequate supervision, and sport safety awareness information to participants, family members, and workers.

We believe that the frequency and severity of accidents in sport and recreation activities can be reduced through attention to a number of issues:

- Provide safety educational material about products and activities (e.g., information on proper eye protection in racquet sports).

- Modify the rules by which products may be used or the activity conducted (e.g., disallow bodychecking in company hockey leagues).

- Ban the product or activity or substantially change it (e.g., American Academy of Pediatrics called for the total ban of the trampoline, because it contributed to injuries that resulted in quadriplegia).

- Modify products to reduce hazards associated with them (e.g., provide face masks on hockey helmets).

- Limit the use of the product or participation in the activity to times or places at which injuries are less likely to occur (e.g., use school play equipment only during supervised times).

- Limit product use or activity participation to those people specifically trained or skilled (e.g., require certification of instruction by an authorized organization or individual).

- Enforce better control over players or participants (e.g., ensure that qualified lifeguards are stationed at all public swimming areas).

- Change the environment in which the product is used or activity pursued (e.g., place sand instead of pavement under all playground equipment).

- Develop and use personal protective equipment (e.g., lightweight helmets for recreational skiers).

In this book, we have attempted to address many of the sport and recreation activities that North Americans enjoy on a daily basis. *Safety Sense at Play* is a family reference book that explains why accidents occur and what steps we can take to prevent them. Safety Sense at Play also includes hints on how to reduce the danger of death and serious injury. For each play activity we present the "risk" involved in that activity, the most significant causes of accidents related to the play activity, and the safety sense actions to prevent injury.

Identifying the death and injury rates for the many varied sports and recreational activities within this play safety book was a very difficult task. However, the statistics presented are found primarily in the following reports on accident statistics. In some cases where no other data were available, we relied on individual studies performed by sports medicine physicians, associations, and private researchers:

- U.S. Consumer Product Safety Commision, National Electronic Injury Surveillance System (NEISS)
- Consumer and Corporate Affairs, Canada, Canadian Electronic Injury Surveillance System (CEISS)
- National Safety Council, Accident Facts
- Canada Safety Council, Accident Fatalities
- SPORTSEARCH, Sport Information Resource Centre (SIRC), Gloucester, Ontario, Canada
- Ministry of Tourism and Recreation, Ontario, Canada
- Régie de la sécurité dans les sports du Québec, Québec, Canada.

SNOW AND ICE SPORTS

Common sense, preparation and prevention are the keys to enjoying outdoor winter sports without unpleasant side effects. Parents, coaches, and recreation leaders who are responsible for others can contribute to people's safety by running a safety workshop or giving a brief safety talk before a sporting event. If you ensure that the following safety items are covered, you will contribute to minimizing injuries in winter sports.

- Is appropriate warm clothing available?
- Is personal protective equipment available?
- Do the participants have the necessary skill to participate in the activity?
- Are warm-up exercises done before starting the activity?
- Do participants know the playing rules -- especially the safety ones?
- Is the equipment in good working condition?
- If the activity is outdoors, have weather forecasts been checked?
- Do all participants refrain from using alcohol and/or other drugs?
- Are scheduled rest breaks planned to prevent overexertion and fatigue?

Alpine Skiing

RISK FACTORS
- Novice skiers suffer more injuries than experienced skiers.
- Female skiers are more likely to sustain lower extremity (leg, knee, etc.,) injuries than males.
- Knee ligament injuries account for 20 to 25 percent of all skiing injuries.
- Thumb injuries account for 40 percent of all upper extremity injuries.

CONTRIBUTING FACTORS
- high, stiff boots and some bindings that don't protect the knee from stress
- thumb injuries caused by driving the thumb into the snow on a forward fall
- crashing into other skiers or obstacles on the ski run

COMMENT

Skiing can be a safe sport. Statistics show that on any given day, the skier is exposed to a very low risk of injury. Nonetheless, both the skier and people responsible for the welfare of skiers (chaperons, ski patrollers, and parents) should be aware of the risk of injuries in skiing and should know how to prevent them. Although there are many factors involved in preventing skiing accidents, two stand out above the others. They are the experience of the skier and the type and condition of the ski equipment. Injuries that occur as a result of these two factors can be reduced by taking professional skiing lessons and purchasing or renting properly fitted, properly adjusted, and properly maintained equipment.

SAFETY SENSE

- Ski under control so that you can stop and avoid objects or other skiers.
- Wear ski goggles. The best protection against glare and snowblindness is provided by yellow or smoked lenses, which should be made of polycarbonate material.
- Do not stop where you obstruct a trail or are not visible from above.
- Avoid potential avalanche areas by staying off steep, snow-covered slopes when you are outside developed ski areas. Always ski with a buddy.
- The skier below you always has the right of way.
- Use pre-season physical conditioning and warm-up exercises prior to skiing to help prevent injuries.

- When entering a trail or starting downhill, yield to other skiers.
- Professional instruction should be taken by all beginners.
- All skiers should use a retention system (Arlbergstraps) to prevent runaway skis.
- When you buy second-hand equipment, have it checked by a ski shop or ski professional to ensure that it is in good condition.
- Keep off closed trails and posted areas, and observe all posted signs.
- No matter how experienced you are, wear a ski helmet at all times.
- Protect yourself from frostbite and snow burn by wearing appropriate ski clothing.
- Don't drink alcohol until after the day's skiing is over and the drive home is completed.

Bobsled and Luge

RISK FACTORS

- Most fatalities from bobsled and luge accidents result from injuries to the head and neck.
- Headaches and sore necks are common among bobsledders.
- Most scrapes and bruises result from being rocked about within the sled rather than from collisions or spillovers on the track.
- A good number of injuries (such as muscle strain, pulled hamstrings, and quadriceps injuries) occur during the start-up of the run, when pushing the sled to get it going.
- Between 1983 to 1985 at Mount van Hoevenberg, Lake Placid, there were 13 injuries per 1,000 bobsled runs and 3.8 injuries per 1,000 luge runs.

CONTRIBUTING FACTORS

- poor physical conditioning and failing to warm up well
- using a run without the supervision of a coach, an emergency medical technician, and an ambulance in attendance
- the constant jarring of the sled and excessive speed, which produces a force of nearly 4G

COMMENT

In North America, there are two internationally sanctioned runs -- one in Calgary, Alberta and the other in Lake Placid, New York. Because spills can be dangerous, expert design and special care of the track are of critical importance. Modern bahns are constructed so that when a spill occurs, the user and sled remain in the track, held by the banking of the turns and the retaining lips along the top of the track.

SAFETY SENSE

- Wear protective equipment, such as goggles, head gear, elbow and knee pads, and shoulder pads.
- Warm up for at least 20 minutes.

- In practice and competition, have emergency medical personnel and ambulance services at the site.

Broomball

RISK FACTORS
- No North American data are available.

CONTRIBUTING FACTORS
- failing to wear protective equipment
- bodychecking other players
- being struck by other players' broomsticks
- falls

COMMENT

Broomball is similar to ice hockey, except that a 25 cm (10 in.) rubber ball is used instead of a puck and the players do not use skates. The injuries sustained while playing broomball are also similar to those that happen in hockey. Most injuries occur from being tripped; bodychecked; cross-checked with the stick; hit with a slash, a high stick, or a thrown broom; or elbowed in the head or face.

SAFETY SENSE

- Don't allow bodychecking.
- Never use a whip shot (moving the broom above the shoulders in a windmill-like action).
- Cover brooms with plastic and tape them from handle to tip.
- Wear the following protective equipment: helmet, elbow and knee pads, proper footwear, gloves, and hip and shin pads.
- Players penalized for any violation of the rules should be given a warning, and any player who violates the rules for a second time should be ejected from the game.

Cross-Country Skiing

RISK FACTORS
- Cross-country skiing is one of the safest winter sports; it has an estimated injury rate of 0.2 to 0.7 injuries per 1,000 skier days.

CONTRIBUTING FACTORS
- impact with snow surface because of a fall
- colliding with an object such as a tree or rock
- twisting body parts
- colliding with another person
- falling on a ski pole
- overuse of muscles causing strains
- failing to do pre-conditioning and warm-up exercises
- hypothermia and frostbite
- skiers' inexperience

COMMENT

If you really want to get away from all the hustle and bustle of life, go cross-country skiing or nordic skiing, as it is sometimes referred to. Besides providing you with the opportunity to ski far from the crowds and get back to nature, cross-country skiing is good exercise and an inexpensive sport.

SAFETY SENSE

- Participate in a pre-season conditioning program, and always do 20 minutes of warm-up exercises, especially arm and leg stretches.
- Ski with a "buddy".
- Don't tackle a trail that is too tough for you.
- Use a map and ski on recognized trails.
- Notify others of your intended route.
- Wear clothing that will allow for ventilation and still retain heat. Ask your sport store about appropriate clothing types.
- If you are skiing for more than a couple of hours, take food and drink. On longer trips, carry extra clothing.
- Be prepared for accidents, emergencies, or damaged equipment by carrying a repair kit, a ski tip, and a first-aid kit.
- Check your partner's condition frequently. Watch for signs of frostbite, hypothermia, and fatigue.
- Regroup at intersections to ensure that everyone follows the same route.

- Take several short breaks rather than a few long ones. This will prevent overexertion injuries.
- Don't ski too close to your companions; it is annoying and could cause an accident.
- On blind descents, call a warning to skiers who might be on the hill. When you have reached the bottom, call to waiting skiers that the trail is clear.
- Roll off the track as soon as possible after a fall and even out the snow for the next skier.
- Always ski with caution, watching out for open streams and fallen trees.
- Avoid snow-covered lakes.
- Know the location of snowmobile trails, and show courtesy toward snowmobilers -- they may save your life one day!

Curling

RISK FACTORS
- No North American data are available.

CONTRIBUTING FACTORS
- slips and falls
- overuse of muscles
- strained muscles from sweeping and stone (rock) delivery

COMMENT

Curling is an ice sport of fitness and finesse enjoyed by thousands of North Americans. Like golf, curling is a lifetime sport. It's played for both recreation and competitive satisfaction by men and women of all ages. It may be the safest of winter sports, but players should approach it in ways that are appropriate for their age and physical condition. Curling requires a certain degree of fitness due to the vigorous sweeping, the length of the game, and the walking required, so pre-season conditioning and good warm-up exercises before the game is very important.

SAFETY SENSE

- While sweeping the stone (rock), be careful not to trip over it.
- Stay well back from the center play area when not sweeping to avoid colliding with other sweepers.
- Warm up before or during a curling match to get yourself psychologically ready for the game, to keep warm, to improve your flexibility (this will decrease the chance of injury and smooth out your delivery when throwing a stone), and to diminish the chance of a heart attack or stroke.
- Social drinking should take place only when the day's matches are over.

RISK FACTORS

- Injury rates for bodychecking leagues are four times higher than for non-bodychecking leagues.
- Some 70 to 80 percent of fractures to the head, neck, or shoulder are caused from physical contact by the opponent.
- Hockey sticks account for about 18 percent of hockey injuries.
- Most injuries occur to persons aged 15 to 24; five to 14-year-olds are next.

CONTRIBUTING FACTORS

- being hit by a stick, puck, or other player's protective equipment
- colliding with goal posts
- bodychecking
- going head first into the boards
- getting pushed or checked from behind
- being cut by skate blade

COMMENT

Hockey has always been a sport in which the potential for injury is high. Over the last 20 to 25 years, the chance and seriousness of injuries have increased because the players have become bigger, they skate faster, and they hit and shoot the puck harder. In addition, the marked improvement of protective equipment over the last 20 to 25 years has made the participants less aware of the dangers of the game. Players often play the game with reckless abandon, not hesitating to dive in front of pucks or skate at full speed toward the end boards. Players use their sticks to slow down the opposition. Combine all these factors, and the risk of injury becomes high indeed. It is safest to play recreational hockey in a league that does not allow body contact.

SAFETY SENSE

- When buying a hockey helmet or face protector, make sure it carries the Canadian Standards Association (CSA) or the American Society of Testing and Materials (ASTM) mark.
- Goalie moulded masks, especially those not custom-made to fit the face, do not provide adequate protection.

- Do not wash your helmet and face mask with anything except a mild detergent. Abrasive cleaning substances may scratch the mask, and solvents will weaken the helmet structure.
- Do not put decals on your helmet; they may hide a crack in the helmet.
- The wearing of proper and well-fitting protective equipment is an absolute must. You need the following protective equipment: helmet, face guard, throat guard, mouth guard, elbow/shoulder pads, pants, protective cup, shin guards, and gloves. The equipment must fit well and be appropriate for your caliber of play. Repair or replace any piece that is not in good condition.
- Stay aware of where your opponents are so you can avoid checks and collisions.
- When taking a bodycheck along the boards, use your hands and arms as a cushion; keep your head up; and turn your body so your shoulders hit first. Stay close to the boards: don't get caught in the danger zone 1.2 m (2 to 4 ft.) from the boards.
- Coaches, officials, and parents must insist that all levels of hockey be played according to the rules of the game and of fair play. Make sure that the rink has properly maintained emergency medical equipment available. Establish a precise emergency protocol to be followed in the event of a serious injury. Have properly qualified medical, paramedical, or training personnel on hand during all team activities. Tell players about the dangers of the game, and teach them the proper ways to reduce the risk of injury (e.g., pre-game stretching to reduce the likelihood of strains, neck strengthening exercises to reduce the incidence and severity of spinal injury).

Iceboating

RISK FACTORS
- No North American data are available.

CONTRIBUTING FACTORS
- speeding too fast for conditions
- stunting (horseplay)
- colliding with other boats
- inexperienced operators

COMMENT

An iceboat in winds of 40 km/h (25 mph) can move along at speeds up to 160 km/h (100 mph). The speed demands good judgment and skilled iceboat operators.

SAFETY SENSE

- Wear thermal or woollen underwear, windproofed outergarments, gloves or mittens that are warm and flexible, and footwear that is warm and provides good traction. Goggles or face masks will help prevent frostbite, and a helmet is a good investment.
- For greatest safety, select sites that are large in area so that a safe distance can be kept between boats.
- Carefully check your course before attaining high speeds. Look for cracked or heaved ice, snow drifts, open water, and obstacles such as fishing huts and frozen tree stumps.
- Carry an emergency box with extra clothing, first-aid materials, rope, emergency food, and flares.
- Carry liability insurance on your ice craft.
- Read your boat's operating manual thoroughly.
- Observe the same rules of the road on ice as you would on a highway.
- If you are a beginner, keep your boat's speed within your capabilities to control. Leave "hiking" (performing stunts on the ice) until you become more proficient.
- Don't ever "skin" (just miss) another craft.

Ice Fishing

RISK FACTORS

- No North American data are available. However, insurance reports show that some 600 vehicles plunge through the ice each year, often taking passengers to their death.

CONTRIBUTING FACTORS

- falling through the ice
- failing to wear proper clothing for weather conditions
- failing to use a buddy system
- failing to constantly measure ice thickness
- fishing on unfamiliar ice surfaces

COMMENT

Ice fishing is a popular winter activity and an inexpensive sport that can be enjoyed by the whole family. There are several methods of practicing this ancient pastime; you can use jigging lines with lures or bait, bait sets with tip-ups, bait sets with bobbers, or a fish spear.

The most important safety factor in ice fishing is the thickness of the ice. Can it withstand the weight of a person, a snowmobile, or a car? Here are some guidelines for determining if the ice is safe: 5 cm (2 in.) thick, one person can walk on it; 8 cm (3 in.), three people can walk across it in single file; 15 cm (6 in.), all-terrain vehicles and snowmobiles can travel safely; and 20 cm (8 in.) ice should support a motor vehicle. If the ice is on a river, remember that currents affect the thickness. Small ponds freeze faster than large open bodies of water. It is always a good idea to ask advice from local fishermen and fishing store operators.

SAFETY SENSE

- Boots must be insulated and waterproof. Keep boots loosely tied so they can be kicked off if you fall into the water.
- Wear sunglasses to prevent snow-blindness.
- Consider wearing a lifejacket or vest under your outer clothing.
- Take along survival items such as waterproof matches, chocolate bars, a transistor radio for weather reports, and extra socks and mitts.

- When walking on the ice, look out for half-frozen or open holes left by other fishermen.
- Stay away from protruding rocks or pilings frozen in the ice. The ice is weaker around these objects.
- If walking, use a sled to distribute weight over the ice. If you break through, the extra length of the sled may prevent it from going through the hole and help you get out.
- Follow paths made by other vehicles or people.
- If you are going fishing on an unfamiliar river, don't do it unless you can see other fishermen or their trails.
- On large lakes, take a compass with you. A quick snow storm could eliminate your landmarks.
- Fish with a buddy and tie a 9 m (30 ft.) rope between you. This is your lifeline.
- When driving on ice, all windows should be rolled down completely. The doors should be left ajar and no seat belts fastened. Leave ten vehicle lengths between vehicles.
- Do not park vehicles near each other. Spread them out at least 60 m (200 ft.) from each other.

- If you have a stove in your shanty, ensure that it is well ventilated to prevent carbon monoxide poisoning.
- Anchor your hut deeply into the ice at all four corners. Runaway huts are a hazard.
- If you are using an axe, chisel, or auger to make a hole, keep bystanders well back. Chips of ice can injure an eye.
- Be especially careful when using augers. The blades are dangerously sharp. Put the guards back onto the blades when they are not being used.
- If you fall through the ice, don't panic and thrash about. Most people can survive in cold water for about 25 minutes. Your immediate concern is to keep from drowning. Generally your winter clothes will provide enough buoyancy to keep your face out of the water. Break ice around you until you find some that is solid enough to pull yourself out. Once out, lay spreadeagled on the ice and slide or roll until you are well clear of the hole.
- Once you have finished with a hole, put snow in it and mark it with a stick for the safety of others.

Ice-Skating

RISK FACTORS

- Over 25,000 people are treated each year in North America for injuries received while recreational ice-skating.
- Injuries are highest among people aged 11 to 25 years.

CONTRIBUTING FACTORS

- falls
- colliding with other skaters
- tripping on irregular ice surfaces
- cuts from skate blades
- drowning

COMMENT

Ice is a hazard to motorists and pedestrians, but to skaters, ice is a dance floor, a race track, or a playing field. You can enjoy ice skating in public supervised rinks or on rivers, ponds, and lakes. But whatever area you choose, consider these safety sense tips.

SAFETY SENSE

- Proper clothing is essential for outdoor recreational skating. You should wear long pants, thermal underwear in very cold weather, heavy mittens, and a toque or some other hat.
- Properly fitted skates will increase your skating ability and help prevent mishaps.
- After a fall on the ice, be sure to pull both arms in toward the body to avoid being cut by another's skate blade.

In Rinks
- Observe the posted rules. In most rinks, such activities as races and unorganized games (tag, crack the whip, long jump) are prohibited during public skating. Unless a special area is set aside, hockey, figure skating, and ice dancing should be avoided also.
- Take children to rinks that are supervised.

Ponds, Rivers, and Lakes
- The ice must be at least 5 cm (2 in.) thick for one skater and 8 cm (3 in.) thick for three. Ice that is 10 cm (4 in.) thick is safe for groups of skaters.
- Never skate alone on a lake, pond, or river.

- Skate with people who are familiar with the skating area.
- Do not skate in the late spring since the ice begins to melt from underneath at this time of year.
- Skate on a surface that has a depth of no more than 1 to 1½ m (3 to 5 ft.) of water beneath it.
- Beware of crystallized ice.
- Beware of refrozen surfaces. These can be very dangerous because the ice might appear solid but really be weak.
- Be cautious of snow covering the ice surface. Due to the weight of the snow, hairline cracks may appear in the ice, increasing the danger of breaking through the surface.
- If you fall through the ice, don't panic and thrash about. Most people can survive in cold water for about 25 minutes. Your immediate concern is to keep from drowning. Generally your winter clothes will provide enough buoyancy to keep your face out of the water. Break ice around you until you find some that is solid enough to pull yourself out. Once out, you should lay spread-eagled on the ice and slide or roll until you are well clear of the hole.
- When group or family skating, take along a 9 m (30 ft.) rope just as a precaution. Other devices that can assist you in getting out of the water are a knife or special gloves with picks mounted into the palms.
- Children should be allowed to skate only in supervised areas with a buddy -- never alone. They should be taught to stay close to the edge of the shore where the water is shallow.
- Do not build warming fires on the ice.

Ringette

RISK FACTORS
- Fourteen percent of all reported injuries are to the face.
- Strains and bruises account for the majority of injuries in ringette.
- Extremities are vulnerable to bruises caused by collisions and stick contact.
- Improper or poorly fitting equipment can cause injury.

CONTRIBUTING FACTORS
- lack of a good warm-up
- improper technique or lack of skill
- careless attitude while competing
- not being in proper physical condition to participate in a fast-moving sport
- not wearing suitable equipment or wearing equipment improperly

COMMENT

Ringette is a non-contact sport invented in 1963. Its evolution continues to alter the equipment requirements for participants. Throughout its existence, ringette has always been classified as a low-risk sport; however, as the skill of players rapidly advances and the speed of the game increases, there are now more injuries being reported. Injuries that do occur are generally minor.

Ringette emphasizes skating agility, teamwork, and sportsmanship. Players are required to wear certain equipment, while other equipment is optional.

SAFETY SENSE

- Choose proper-fitting equipment suitable for ringette.
- Wear the equipment for all games and practices.
- Mandatory equipment includes a helmet and facemask; elbow pads; padded gloves; hip, tailbone and genital protection; knee pads; and skates. All should be approved by the Canadian Standards Association or the American Society of Testing and Materials.
- Recommended equipment includes throat protection, internal mouth guard, shoulder pads, and shin pads.
- Work to get into shape to play and stay in shape while participating.
- Warm up with gentle exercise prior to playing or practicing.
- Take the time to learn the proper techniques for performing all the skills.
- Participate with your safety and that of other participants in mind.

Ski-Jumping

RISK FACTORS
- At Lake Placid, the injury rate for ski-jumping and World Cup competition ranges from 1.2 to 4.3 injuries per 1,000 skier-days.
- Injury rates are not available for training sessions in North America.

CONTRIBUTING FACTORS
- falls
- incorrect flight position
- poor snow preparation
- inappropriate official judgment of wind conditions and hill conditions

COMMENT

Ski-jumping is unique. Very few sports pack such excitement, poise, finesse, and occasional glory into so few seconds. Ski-jumping flourishes in communities where local ski-jumping clubs and hills are available. Most jumpers begin at age seven or eight on small hills. By the time they reach 18, jumpers are ready to qualify for competition. The impression that ski-jumping is excessively dangerous is not true. Ski-jumping is less dangerous than alpine racing.

SAFETY SENSE

- Jumps must be well prepared. A hard, smooth, ice-free surface is essential.
- All jumps must be supervised by a race or hill committee to ensure absolute safety. Jumpers should have the proven ability to handle the hill size.
- Hill supervisors should monitor the wind speed. Wind speed indicators must be strategically placed at the start line and at the takeoff knoll. If the wind is too strong, no one should jump.
- Adequate first-aid coverage is needed at all jump sites.
- Use a helmet. Get the help of a professional when selecting ski clothing, skis, boots, and bindings.
- Horseplay on the hill should not be tolerated.

Sledding

RISK FACTORS
- Over 35,000 people annually are treated in North America for injuries received while sliding down hills.
- Over 20 percent of all sledding-related injuries involve concussion, internal injury, or broken bones.
- Forty percent of all injuries occur to children aged five to nine.
- The average hospital stay for serious sledding injuries is six to eight days.

CONTRIBUTING FACTORS
- running into a fixed object
- falling from the sled
- colliding with another sled or person
- failing to wear head protection

COMMENT

A sled, toboggan, snow racer, or tube on a snow-covered hill offers the thrill of earth-bound flight. Hopping on a sled or tube and zooming downhill can be fun, but it can also be very risky. Most often sledding activities are unsupervised and hill rules are not followed.

SAFETY SENSE

- Choose a hill that is clear of obstacles and has a long run at its base. Many communities have hills that are maintained for sledding. Use them.
- Stay off hills that are ice-covered or have tree stumps, rocks, or bare spots.
- Before leaving for the hill, check all equipment for cracks, splinters, etc.
- Always wear a helmet when sledding. This inexpensive protective device would prevent most serious injuries.
- Never slide with a long scarf dangling. It could get caught on something and strangle you.
- First-time sledders need instructions and should start on small, gentle slopes.
- Never let children slide down slopes towards a street.
- Small children should never go sledding unsupervised.
- Never stand up on a sled or toboggan.
- Never pile on more people than the sled was designed for. Most sledding equipment, except for a toboggan, should carry only one rider.
- If a collision is going to happen, roll sideways off the sled and protect your head with your hands and arms.
- When at the end of your run, move quickly off to the side to avoid collision with other sledders coming down the hill.
- Always walk up the hill well off the sledding path.

Snowboarding

RISK FACTORS

- No North American data are available, although the increased popularity of this sport will probably lead sport associations and hospitals to collect injury data in the near future.

CONTRIBUTING FACTORS

- falls
- crashing into other snowboarders, skiers, and obstacles
- knee sprains and strains from twisting the legs and body

COMMENT

A combination of surfing, skiing, skateboarding, and windsurfing, snowboarding has recently become a very popular sport on the ski hills. After some crude designs in the mid-1960s, the present snowboard, with its steel edges and highback bindings, provides for much more control. Its use is now accepted at many ski resorts, a number of which offer professional instruction and even certification programs.

SAFETY SENSE

- Make sure you rent or purchase a snowboard that has full-length steel edges and stiff, secure bindings. Both are required for good control.
- Footwear selection will depend on your binding system; however, proper fit is very important to prevent injury.
- The best place to learn this activity is at a snowboarding school. Practice on small hills and on soft snow.
- If you are a beginner, go slow and concentrate on developing your turning skill. This approach will prevent many needless falls and possible injuries.
- To use ski lifts, enter the left loading area. Take your back foot out of the binding and push the board like a skateboard. After getting off the lift, glide down the ramp with your rear foot on the board.
- Snowboarders also should follow the safety sense advice given in the section on alpine skiing.

Snow Caving

RISK FACTORS
- No North American data are available.

CONTRIBUTING FACTORS
- suffocation
- carbon-monoxide poisoning
- hypothermia
- body chill as a result of sweating and cooling down

COMMENT

For experienced campers looking for new adventures, snow caving can be an enjoyable recreational experience. It can also provide excellent emergency shelter. Snow shelters are warmer and more comfortable to live in than tents. Yet, they are not without their dangers if not constructed properly.

SAFETY SENSE

- Build your cave in a wind-deposited drift around boulders. That way the sides stay in essentially the same position, so there is no danger of having the entrance deeply buried during the night. The leeward side of a steep hill is also a good choice.
- The warmest caves have entrances below the level of the floor, permitting cold air to seep out.
- Drifts that have been packed by the wind are generally more solid than normal fallen snow.
- Always check the thickness of any new, unconsolidated snow on top of the drift before you start digging from below to be sure you don't penetrate into this layer.

- The roof of the cave should be dome-shaped to prevent it from sagging and possibly collapsing during the night.
- It is important not to get wet while digging. Overexertion causes sweating. Damp clothes contribute to hypothermia.
- If you are cooking, a large airhole high in the cave is needed to prevent carbon-monoxide poisoning and to supply air.
- The walls and ceiling should be at least 30 cm (12 in.) thick to provide enough insulation and support.
- Keep candles or lanterns in a secure place, away from flammable materials.

Snowmobiling

RISK FACTORS

- Over 40 percent of all snowmobile collisions involve drivers under the age of 20.
- Approximately 10 percent of all snowmobile collisions involve defective equipment.
- In 30 percent of all snowmobile accidents, the driver had been drinking. Over 40 percent of the fatalities from these accidents involve drinking drivers under the age of 20.
- Not wearing a helmet doubles the chance of a minor head injury, triples the chance of a moderate head injury, and quadruples the chance of a serious head injury.
- Fifty percent of all snowmobile accidents occur at night.
- Eight of ten off-road accidents involve collisions with trees and fences after the driver has lost control of the snowmobile.
- Approximately 10 percent of all snowmobile fatalities are a result of drowning.
- Of road-related accidents, 70 percent occur in the traffic lanes, 30 percent occur on the shoulder or in the ditch area.
- In jurisdictions where permits are required to operate snowmobiles, 20 percent of the drivers do not hold one.
- Twenty percent of snowmobile collisions involve drivers under the age of 16.

CONTRIBUTING FACTORS

- failing to maintain the snowmobile in a safe operating condition
- lack of knowledge of snowmobile safe-riding laws and regulations
- lack of understanding of trail signs
- drinking and driving
- failing to wear a helmet and other protective equipment
- exposed skin (leading to frostbite)
- speeding
- operator inattentiveness
- failing to yield the right-of-way
- driving a snowmobile on a public road or in ditches along the roadside

COMMENT

Snowmobiles are indispensable to professional hunters and trappers, to the residents of northern communities, to foresters, rangers and police officers. However, most snowmobiles are used for recreational purposes. Whatever the use, there is a need for safety sense. A surprising number of people are killed or injured in snowmobile accidents, but our data are culled from only a few states and provinces. We do know that many snowmobile collisions occur on public roads.

SAFETY SENSE

- Maintain your machine in accordance with the manufacturer's owner's manual.
- Ensure that there is a running board for the operator's and passenger's feet.
- Ensure that your machine has the proper lighting and reflectors on it.
- If the throttle sticks, immediately use the emergency shut-off switch.
- When towing a cutter (sleigh), use a snow flap and check passengers frequently. Equip the cutter with reflectors and reflective materials, and ensure that the tow bar is safely secured.
- If you are a beginner, participate in a snowmobile safety course. There are also courses for experienced riders.
- Select a helmet approved by the Canadian Standards Association, the Snell Memorial Foundation, USA Federal Motor Vehicle Safety Standard 218, or the British Standards Institute. A helmet should have a strong chin strap and a plastic protective shield to guard against eye injury and frostbite and to improve your seeing ability.
- Use clothing that ventilates; clothing made especially for snowmobiling is best.
- Do not use ordinary gloves made with straight-cut fingers. The best hand covering is a pair of mittens with the back insulated like a boxing glove to protect your knuckles from the cold.
- Snowmobiler boots are best; however, any boot that has an inner felt liner is suitable. Your feet do sweat, and liners must remain dry to be effective. One pair of woollen socks will be sufficient if liners are dry.
- Only carry passengers on machines that are designed to do so.
- Warn passengers of dangerous obstacles such as uneven ground or low branches.
- Small children should be carried in front of the operator where they will be better warmed and protected.
- Never allow children to operate a snowmobile unless they are trained in its use and are supervised. Don't allow them to travel on or cross a roadway.
- Always ride your snowmobile in off-road areas.
- Snowmobilers must yield the right-of-way to all other motor vehicle traffic on a roadway.
- Never drive on the main portion of a roadway.
- Follow snowmobile trails and use road crossing points that are marked by signs to warn motorists.
- Cross roadways at right angles.

- Always stop before crossing a roadway and make sure that no traffic is coming.
- Road culverts are extremely difficult to spot; drive on the edge of a ditch away from the road.
- A roadway should be crossed within 5 m (15 ft.) of an intersection, at a 90° angle to the intersection.
- Passengers are not allowed to be in a cutter (sleigh) while crossing the roadway.
- It is unsafe to operate a snowmobile without headlights turned on between sunset and sunrise and whenever visibility is reduced.
- Your headlights allow you only a short time to react; drive slowly enough to allow yourself the reaction time you need.
- Moderate speed should be used at all times.
- Don't drink and drive. If drinking is a part of your snowmobiling activities, schedule it for the end of the trip.
- Impaired passengers pose serious safety problems for drivers. Refuse to carry them.
- Keep your body within the width of the machine to protect yourself from dangerous objects such as trees and posts.
- Always use the buddy system on any trip.
- Never travel into unfamiliar territory, and always let someone know where you are going and when you plan to return.
- Avoid unfamiliar lakes and rivers. Check with informed officials, such as conservation officers or police officers, or measure the thickness of ice on lakes and rivers before you drive on them.
- Respect the property and rights of others and don't litter the trails.
- Shut off the engine before scooping snow from under the track.
- Cross railway tracks with extreme caution. Aside from the obstacles of the tracks and track ties, anytime is train time.
- All accidents involving personal injury, death, or damage to property belonging to another person must be reported to the police.

Snowshoeing

RISK FACTORS
- No North American data are available.

CONTRIBUTING FACTORS
- hypothermia
- drowning
- snowslides
- overexertion

COMMENT

History suggests that the first snowshoes were used when someone fastened crude wooden slats to their feet and walked across deep snow. Today, snowshoes are used by ranchers, foresters, and utility linemen, as well as by people seeking outdoor winter recreation. Although there are some who say snowshoeing is nothing but hard work, many people have welcomed it as an inexpensive and peaceful winter entertainment.

SAFETY SENSE

- Always go snowshoeing with a buddy.
- Carry a ski pole to test snow that might start a snowslide if you stepped on it.
- Walk naturally to prevent muscle strain.
- For comfort, wear loose but warm clothing, goggles, and waterproof boots.
- Plan your trip and tell relatives or friends where you are going.
- Carry emergency supplies, such as waterproof matches, energy food, extra clothing, and a first aid kit.
- Seek the advice of a professional when buying or renting snowshoes.
- Avoid crossing streams if you can. If you must cross a stream, be especially careful to test the ice at the crossing point.

Speed-Skating

RISK FACTORS

- No North American data are available. Most injuries occur during off-ice training -- low back pain and knee pain from weightlifting, muscle pulls and tendonitis from running and cycling, and bumps and contusions from bicycle accidents.

CONTRIBUTING FACTORS

- hand injuries and bruises from falls
- boot-related injuries
- lacerations and stab wounds from skate blades
- muscle strain
- frostbite and hypothermia
- lung injuries from breathing cold air

COMMENT

Recreational speed-skating is almost injury-free and so is competitive racing. The most demanding part of the sport for competitive racers arises from the physical and psychological results of training many hours a day, travel, and living away from home.

SAFETY SENSE

- Reduce the chance of foot injuries by ensuring that you have adequate boot padding and properly fitted skates. Tighten your skates carefully.
- Warm up well, especially in very cold weather, to help prevent muscle strain.
- To prevent frostbite during training, wear warm clothing; use face masks, mittens rather than gloves, and skate covers. Take frequent warming breaks while training outside in extremely cold conditions.
- Wear cut-resistant mittens to prevent hand injuries.
- Wear protective equipment during training, especially if you are a beginner. Equipment should include helmet, kneepads, gloves, and elbow pads.
- Maintain your skate blades and boots.
- Injury may occur at the start of a sprint race when a skate blade cuts the skater's opposite leg. Professional coaching and training will generally prevent this type of injury.
- Overtraining can be a serious problem, especially for young inexperienced skaters, so ensure that adequate rest periods are provided.
- If using a lake or a river for training, ensure that the ice thickness is at least 8 cm (3 in.).
- Attach skate blade guards to your skate blades when not on the ice surface.

COURT SPORTS

Although floor sports, such as badminton, racquetball, squash, and volleyball, differ markedly in playing environment, technique, and skill demands, they place many similar physical stresses on the athlete and share a common potential for certain injuries.

The most common contributing cause of court injuries is the failure of athletes to get into condition and to warm up adequately before participating. These sports demand bursts of muscular activity, repetitive movements of arm and shoulder, and rapid twists and changes of direction, followed by brief periods of rest. This combination of sudden starts and stops on inflexible and weak muscles often results in injury. Although these sports are considered by many participants to be social more than athletic events, preconditioning and warm-up and warm-down exercises are nevertheless vital.

Badminton

RISK FACTORS

- Badminton participation results in few injuries. It is estimated that only some 2,000 people receive medical attention each year in North America for injuries received while playing badminton.
- One study reported that badminton has an average injury rate of 0.12 injuries per person per year.
- Players may suffer blisters, strains, sprains, and badminton elbow, or tendonitis.

CONTRIBUTING FACTORS

- colliding with net or support equipment
- colliding with another person (usually one's partner)
- being struck by a racquet or shuttle
- muscle strain
- slips and falls

COMMENT

Badminton is an entertaining game, whether it is played in the backyard or in an organized club. For the fitness conscious, badminton can tone muscles, develop cardiovascular fitness, and burn off extra calories. It is an inexpensive game; equipment includes a racquet, shuttles, a net and supports, and a flat surface to play on. Local clubs are available in almost every community.

SAFETY SENSE

- If you play competitive badminton, you need to attain a high level of physical conditioning before beginning to play.
- Warm-up exercises that stretch all the muscles and tendons will help reduce muscle strains.
- If you play competitively, select shoes that fit snugly. A good fit includes a footbed contoured for foot support, a sole made of gum rubber to prevent slipping, good ventilation, extra support on the lateral side of the foot, and a rigid heel with a raised sole border to help reduce foot/knee pain and joint injuries caused by the shock of impact.
- Wear sports safety goggles for eye protection.
- When playing with a partner, ensure that you both know what court area you are responsible for to avoid collisions.
- Wipe up all moisture from the playing surface immediately to prevent slips and falls.
- If guide wires are used to support the net posts, be aware of their location and potential hazards.

Basketball

RISK FACTORS

- It is estimated that every year in North America 23 percent of all high school and college basketball players incur injuries that require the players to stop the activity for one or more days.
- It is estimated that over 535,000 people receive medical attention each year in North America for injuries received while playing organized and informal basketball.

CONTRIBUTING FACTORS

- colliding between players
- poor physical conditioning
- unnecessary roughness (elbowing, hip checks, undercutting other players in the air, tripping, and shoving)
- poor officiating
- improper personal protective equipment
- slippery floors (dirt and sweat)
- inadequate play areas
- unsportsmanlike conduct of spectators and players

COMMENT

Basketball is considered a non-contact game, but at some point in its history it lost this characteristic, so that today there is a great deal of contact and very little protective equipment to help players avoid injuries. The participant requires great endurance and good physical conditioning to play safely. Whether playing pickup basketball at the local playground or participating in an organized league, players should observe the following basic safety sense.

SAFETY SENSE

- You should have well-fitted shoes specifically designed for basketball. The shoe should have a nonslip tread, adequate ventilation, and shock-absorbing material under the heel, transverse and longitudinal arch of the foot. The properly fitted shoe is the most important personal item of the basketball player.
- A thin pair of socks under the regular sweat socks will help prevent blisters. To further lessen the risk of blisters, especially in early season workouts, liberally powder the feet

to reduce friction inside the shoe and between the two pairs of socks. Running barefoot in sand before practice will toughen the skin on the bottom of your feet.

- If you need corrective lenses, you should wear firmly secured safety lenses. Contact lenses are an even better choice, since they reduce the risk of serious eye injury from broken glasses. If you don't wear either of the above, wear a protective guard over your glasses.
- All jewelry should be removed when playing.
- Trunks should be equipped with light hip pads.
- Padded knee guards help eliminate floor, pavement, or cement burns and bruises.
- If you have weak knees, seek medical advice on strengthening procedures.
- Make sure you have warm-up clothing to wear during pre-game drills and practice.
- Running before the beginning of organized practice will help improve endurance, condition legs, and reduce the possibility of strained muscles. Warm-ups before pick-up games are also a good idea.
- If you are a woman, wear a brassiere that fits well.
- Clean debris, rocks, and sand from outdoor courts to prevent slips and falls. If outdoor courts are unsuitable for playing, report the problem to your community parks and recreation department, or whoever is responsible for maintenance.

Handball

RISK FACTORS

- It is estimated that 4,300 people receive medical attention each year in North America for injuries received while playing handball.
- Although handball injury studies vary in their findings, generally about 20 percent of all injuries are finger sprains; 30 percent are ankle sprains; 20 percent result from overuse of muscles (strains); 15 percent are hand, shoulder, and arm injuries; and 10 percent are knee injuries.
- Eye injuries are relatively uncommon since the majority of handball players now wear eye protection.

CONTRIBUTING FACTORS

- being struck in the eye by a ball or a hand
- striking the wall with a hand or upper arm
- blows to the head from collisions with other players or walls
- slips and falls
- dehydration or heatstroke
- improperly diving for the ball
- reckless play

COMMENT

Handball is said to be the oldest game played with a ball. The game as it is played today is of Celtic origin. It is a game in which two, three, or four players at a time can play. All you need are a rubber ball, a pair of sneakers, a pair of handball gloves, a wall, and, most important, eye protection.

SAFETY SENSE

- Read and follow the rules of the game. Generally, if you follow the rules, you will minimize chances of injury.
- Before each match, do warm-up exercises, especially for your hands, arms, and shoulders.

- If you are a frequent player of handball, it is important to keep yourself in good physical condition.
- To prevent blisters, make sure you select properly fitted footwear. Two pairs of socks can help minimize any foot discomfort.

- Hand gloves are a good idea for preventing injuries. If you are a beginner, you may wish to use soft sponges in the gloves until your hands are conditioned.
- Because you come into close contact with the walls of a court, be aware of the high risk of hitting your hand against the wall on the backswing or follow-through.
- At no time should you enter a handball court without eye protection. Eye wear must meet the Canadian Standards Association (CSA) or the American Society of Testing and Materials (ASTM) specifications.
- Make sure the court door is secured shut on indoor courts to prevent injury from collisions with it.
- To prevent collisions when learning the game or playing with new partners, it is important to understand how to negotiate for playing space.
- While it is natural to watch the ball at all times, if you are in front of the ball while it is being played by your opponent, do not turn around to see where the ball has gone after you have hit it. By doing this you will prevent eye injuries. After you have made a shot, it is your responsibility to get out of the way of your opponent.
- Keep the ball dry. A wet ball can act unpredictably, causing injury.
- Take a break between games and during the game if necessary, particularly if the court temperature is higher than 26° C (80° F). Resting will prevent heat stroke. Drink plenty of fluids to prevent dehydration.
- When playing team handball, expect that the game play will be rougher and that injuries will occur more frequently because of the increased possibility of collisions with other players.

Racquetball

RISK FACTORS

- Before 1986, the risk of serious eye injury to an unprotected player who played three days a week for 25 years was about 25 percent. Many clubs now make it mandatory to wear eye protection on their courts. This requirement has reduced eye injuries considerably.

CONTRIBUTING FACTORS

- failing to wear eye protection
- being hit by a racquet
- failing to keep your eye on the ball at all times
- colliding with other players and walls
- overexertion

COMMENT

A growing number of eye injuries in the 1970s triggered research on eye protectors for racquetball and similar sports. Research showed that lenseless eye guards were ineffective and that the frames of some lensed eye guards shattered when hit by a ball. Canadian and U.S. organizations have developed standards for eye protectors, requiring that the devices protect the eye from a ball travelling at 145 kmh (90 mph). A variety of eye guards are now available to the consumer. The polycarbonate type seems to be the best lens material. There is no substitute for approved eye guards and sensible, safe playing rules.

SAFETY SENSE

- Wear only eye protection approved by the Canadian Standards Association (CSA) or American Society for Testing and Materials (ASTM). Eye protectors should be comfortable and snugly fit your face. They should be worn with a support strap and be fog resistant. Protectors should also have temple guards in case of an errant swing by you or your partner.
- Select shoes with gum rubber soles to help prevent slips and falls.

- Be constantly alert to your position in relation to your partner's position and develop a strategy to avoid contact.
- Position yourself behind and to one side of your partner to avoid being hit by a racquet.
- Practice good sportsmanship on the court by allowing your partner unobstructed access to return your hit.
- During practice and warm-ups, use only one ball on the court.

- Keep your eye on the ball, but at the moment your opponent hits the ball, turn your face away from the back of the court to avoid being hit on the side or front of the head by a returned ball.
- Make sure you use a safety string on the racquet that is securely fixed to your wrist.
- Don't slam the ball with your racquet if you are frustrated or angry. Behavior such as this results in unexpected injuries.

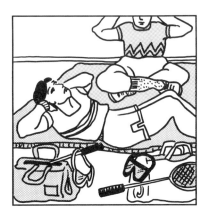

RISK FACTORS

- It is estimated that 3.5 percent of squash players are injured each year.

CONTRIBUTING FACTORS

- failing to wear approved eye protection
- being hit in the face or head by an opponent's racquet
- falling and crashing into walls, door, or door handle of door left ajar
- colliding with opponent
- reckless playing
- wet playing surface

COMMENT

Squash was invented in England during the mid-19th century. The name "squash" originated from the sound the ball made as it was hit against the walls. In addition, the ball was softer or "squashier" than other balls used in court sports. The fact that the game is played at high speed by two or four players in an enclosed area means that the chances of injury from a speeding ball, racquets, and collisions are more likely than in other racquet sports such as tennis or badminton.

For years, squash had a serious eye injury problem. In fact, next to ice hockey, squash had more eye injuries than any other sport. However, with the development of CSA and ASTM specifications for eye protection in racquet sports, eye injuries have been significantly reduced.

SAFETY SENSE

- Never go onto a court without proper eye protection. Select eye guards that have a polycarbonate lens for the best protection.
- To prevent muscle strain, warm up before and warm down after every match.
- If you are over 40 years of age, go for a physical examination by a sports oriented physician first and continue to have a checkup annually.
- Use proper, well-fitted shoes, racquet grips or gloves, and cotton socks to help prevent blisters.
- If you are a beginner, you should wear white or pastel-colored clothing; dark clothing is a poor backdrop against which to see a dark ball.

- Keep racquets in good repair. Handlegrips should be replaced if they have become smooth.
- Wipe up any moisture on the floor immediately to prevent slips and falls.
- Never leave personal items such as watches or jewelry in the court corners where they might be stepped on.
- Make sure that the court door is closed and door handle is flush with the wall.
- Always follow the rules; they are written with safety in mind.
- Keep your eyes on the ball as it comes off the wall and onto your opponent's racquet. It is a common fault to stare at the front waiting for the ball return, then momentarily turn around and get hit by the ball.
- Players should be discouraged from using the technique of "turning." ("Turning" involves following the ball into one of the corners, usually the backhand corner, letting it go around the corner, then hitting it with full force down the middle of the court). While legal, it is extremely dangerous.
- Drink plenty of fluids and take rest breaks between games to prevent or alleviate leg or other types of cramps.

Tennis

RISK FACTORS
- It is estimated that 25,000 people are treated annually at hospital facilities in North America for injuries received while playing tennis.
- Studies show that half of the players who play regularly (two hours per day) will suffer from tennis elbow (soreness in the elbow).

CONTRIBUTING FACTORS
- heatstroke
- the ball striking a player
- running into court fixtures such as net supports
- falls
- carelessness

COMMENT

Tennis is a sport you can enjoy for a lifetime, no matter what your age. The sport promotes both endurance and speed conditioning while simultaneously enhancing balance and agility. While injuries do occur, they could all nearly be eliminated with some common safety sense while on the court.

SAFETY SENSE

- Do warm-up exercises before each match to prevent muscle strain and pulls.
- Always have an adequate supply of water available during the game, especially on sunny and humid days.
- Wear safety glasses. They are inexpensive to buy and prevent eye injury.
- Be aware of the side and back distances to the boundary fence to avoid potentially serious injuries caused by running into the fence.
- Never jump over the net.
- If you are playing doubles, keep an eye on your partner's position to avoid collisions or injuries from swinging racquets.
- Carry a towel to keep your grip-handle dry. Have a new grip put on the racquet if it is worn. A racquet with a worn or wet grip can slip out of your hand and hit another player.
- Make sure your racquet has the proper grip size, weight, and string tightness. This will help prevent arm or shoulder muscle soreness (tennis elbow or tennis shoulder). If such soreness begins to develop, consult your physician.
- Never hit a ball when your opponent is not looking.
- Do not have too many balls spread all over the court. Use a ball basket.
- Clean water and dirt off the court to prevent slips and falls.

Volleyball

RISK FACTORS

- It is estimated that over 102,000 people receive medical attention each year in North America for injuries received while playing organized and informal volleyball.
- One study reports that injuries occurring while performing blocks and spikes outnumber all other sources of injury by a ratio of three to one.

CONTRIBUTING FACTORS

- uncontrolled pursuit of the ball
- uncontrolled jump by a blocker or a spiker
- improper techniques for landing on the court surface
- fatigue
- being hit by the ball
- unsafe equipment such as nets with bolts protruding from supports
- colliding between players and support equipment
- moisture from sweat on the floor

COMMENT

Volleyball today is played by about 50 million people worldwide. It is a game in which two teams volley a ball in the air, back and forth over a net. Volleyball can be played on outdoor courts, in gymnasiums, on beaches, or in backyards. To prevent injuries, the playing surface should be flat and free of debris, with at least 3 m (10 ft.) of safety space beyond the court dimensions for out-of-bound recovery.

SAFETY SENSE

- Before the start of each match, remind all players of the hazards created by support posts, guide wires that support the net, and, if used, officiating stands.
- Stay within your own area of play to prevent collisions with teammates.
- If you play in an organized league, make sure you know safe techniques for diving for the ball and rolling.
- Any time you see moisture on the playing surface, signal for time out to clean it up to prevent slips and falls.
- When blocking and spiking, be careful not to become entangled in the net. Do not attempt to spike a ball that is set too close to the net.
- Keep your eyes on the ball at all times during the game. A volleyball can gain speed well over 100 km/h (60 mph) and can cause serious injury if it hits you.

INDOOR RECREATION

People are gregarious by nature. They like to congregate in small or large groups to socialize -- to talk, laugh, observe, or participate. Indoor recreational activities, many of which are social in nature (dance, aerobics, darts, and so on), rely on the interaction between individuals in order to succeed.

Many indoor recreational activities spring from the idea that sports should be playful and non-competitive. For the most part, the activities require little equipment or financial outlay. These types of activities have the advantage that everyone can participate and benefit.

Aerobics

RISK FACTORS

- Over 30,000 people annually are treated in North America for injuries received while performing aerobic activities.

CONTRIBUTING FACTORS

- insufficient warm-up of muscles before exercising
- overexertion
- slips and falls

COMMENT

Classes in aerobic workouts or dance are a popular form of exercise; many people find aerobics an effective and enjoyable way to burn calories and tone muscles. But as more and more North Americans jump for leaner bodies and healthier hearts, many soon find themselves hobbling around with shin splints, strained ligaments, and sore knees. This doesn't mean, of course, that you should avoid aerobic exercise; it does mean you should avoid overdoing it. The biggest cause of injuries is doing too much, too soon, too often.

SAFETY SENSE

- Before joining an aerobics class, check the instructor's background. Instructors without training in physiology may not understand how physical exercise can inadvertently cause you to have an injury.
- Choose an instructor who teaches aerobic exercise rather than merely performing it. A good instructor monitors her or his students to ensure that the exercises are properly performed.
- Look for an instructor who doesn't try to make everyone conform. If the instructor wants everyone to do 20 repetitions but you feel like doing only 10, you should not be forced to overextend yourself.
- Do not start out in aerobics by buying a home workout video. Beginners need competent instructors to prevent injury-inducing mistakes.
- Listen to your body. Pain is a sign from your body that you are doing too much or doing something incorrectly. A little fatigue after a workout is normal, but if you're still tired two days later, you know you overdid it.

- If you experience any signs of dizziness, chest pains, nausea, or loss of coordination, stop exercising immediately.
- Wear proper footwear to prevent stress on your joints. Shoes should provide cushioning under the ball of the foot, good arch support, and side-to-side support to prevent twisted ankles.
- The best surface to work out on is a raised wooden floor, which absorbs shocks in your joints better than a concrete floor.
- Avoid straight-leg lifts while on your back. Despite common beliefs, they are not good for strengthening the abdominal muscles. Their effect is more on the hip flexors and they place an enormous strain on the lower back area.
- Be careful when doing toe-touches; if your knees are locked, you may hyperextend the back and strain it.
- Avoid hurdler's stretch; it places too much pressure on the ligaments within the knee and can lead to injuries.
- Do not bounce while stretching, especially if you are a beginner. You can easily tear muscle fibres.

Bowling

RISK FACTORS

- It is estimated that approximately 35,000 people receive medical attention each year in North America for injuries received while bowling.

CONTRIBUTING FACTORS

- improper delivery technique
- poor alley etiquette
- moisture on the floor and the alley
- improper method of picking up the ball from the ball-return
- falls

COMMENT

The game of bowling has been played for more than 7,000 years. Objects similar to our modern ten pins were discovered in the grave of an Egyptian whose burial has been dated at 5,200 B.C. In its earliest form, bowling was a crude form of recreation that was played anywhere. Today, we have automatic pin setters and scoring and an excellent choice of balls and equipment. Bowling continues to be a popular and safe sport for all ages.

SAFETY SENSE

- In ten-pin bowling select a ball that fits your finger grip. If the ball is too tight, you will most likely lob it down the alley; if it is too loose, it will drop from your fingers before you intend to release it. A ball of the proper weight will prevent hand injuries such as blisters and tendon damage. Ask for help from the bowling alley personnel.
- You must wear regulation bowling shoes in all alleys. Wearing socks without shoes will cause you to fall on slippery alley floors.
- Wear clothing that is loose and comfortable and allows for freedom of movement.
- Remove debris from the approach to prevent falls. Never deliver a ball if your shoes are wet.
- To prevent finger pinches when picking up a ball from the ball-return, make sure all the balls have stopped moving, keep your hands away from

the ball-return opening, and grasp the ball with both hands.

- Always do a few leg and arm stretching exercises before bowling. Throw a few practice balls to judge lane conditions and to warm up your throwing arm.
- If you are a serious bowler (that is, you bowl two or more times a week), you should perform conditioning exercises for your wrist and arm.
- Never take refreshments into the approach and sitting area. Wetness from spilled drinks on the floor or approach is very dangerous to bowlers.

RISK FACTORS
• It is estimated that some 30,500 people receive medical attention each year in North America for injuries received while dancing.

CONTRIBUTING FACTORS
• stubbing toes, being kicked by other dancers, and jamming toe into the floor
• landing incorrectly from jumps
• sprain and strain of muscles, tendons, and ligaments
• improper footwear
• floor condition
• overexertion
• falls
• failure to perform warm-up exercises
• improper lifting technique
• fatigue

COMMENT

Dance in one form or another has been used to bring harmony to mind and body, performed as part of worship in churches, and practiced simply for the fun of it. There are many forms of dance -- ballet, social, folk, and square. Dancing is a popular recreational activity that requires good self-control and physical poise. The safe performance of dance is largely dependent upon the physical condition of the dancer and the place where the dance is being done.

SAFETY SENSE

• Do warm-up exercises that stretch your muscles. Simply starting the activity slowly is not a good warm-up.
• If you do a great deal of dancing, sports medicine specialists often prescribe swimming as a means of physical conditioning, especially for the lower body (knees, hips, and ankles).
• To prevent shin splints, a soreness that results from swollen tendons pulling away from the shin bone, avoid dancing on hard floors such as cement surfaces. The floor should have a resilient surface, such as linoleum or wood, and should be clear of debris, dust, and moisture to prevent slips and falls.
• To help prevent knee injuries, wear proper shoes, exercise on soft surfaces, and ensure you correctly "turn out" from the hip, not the knee. Knee injuries are generally caused by side-to-side movements and by rapid flexing and extending of the knee joints as in ethnic dance.
• When enrolling in a dance school, ensure that the instructors are certified. Proper instruction can prevent

dance injuries that result from improper landing, jumping, and lifting techniques; improper selection of shoes for the specific type of dance; and improper physical conditioning exercises. Good instructors will also be able to recognize the onset of fatigue or a person who has been injured but continues to dance.

Darts

RISK FACTORS
- No North American data are available.

CONTRIBUTING FACTORS
- stabs (dart punctures)
- overuse of arm muscles
- reckless play

COMMENT

The game of darts is said to have originated in English taverns, with players using the bottom of a wine cask as a target. Today, people all over the world enjoy the game. The darts themselves are dangerous and can cause serious injury. In play, a dart can be thrown wide of the target or can bounce off the board in any direction. Therefore, some safety sense is required when playing the game.

SAFETY SENSE

- Instruct spectators, whether adults at a tournament in a tavern or children watching in the recreation room, to stand well to the side and far back from the board. For home darts, it is a good idea to mark off a safety zone and instruct all dart players and spectators to stay outside this zone.
- Never run and pick up a dart that has fallen to the floor until all players have thrown. Young children, in particular, need to be warned to wait.
- Make sure you don't play for too long at a time. Long periods of practice or throwing the darts too hard can lead to the muscle soreness called "dart throwers' elbow."
- When not using the darts, ensure they are put in a safe place, secured from access by children.
- Adult supervision is required when children play darts. Parents need to determine for themselves when they believe a child has the maturity and safety awareness to play without supervision.

Fencing

RISK FACTORS
- No North American data are available.

CONTRIBUTING FACTORS
- head unprotected
- mask falls off
- mask mesh fails
- mask-bib interface penetrated
- bib-jacket interface penetrated
- blade breaks and penetrates clothing
- recklessness
- poor physical condition

COMMENT

The sport of fencing grew out of duelling, a custom in which sword fighters tried to injure or kill each other. The goal of fencing is not actually to injure but to pretend to wound (to "hit") your opponent and to avoid being hit yourself. Fencing is safe, but only as safe as parents, coaches, officials, and fencers make it. Most beginners instinctively sense the potential dangers involved in fencing and exercise good common sense in protecting themselves and their partners, but for those few who do not, supervision must be provided.

SAFETY SENSE

- Ensure that you are in good physical condition to prevent strains and minor injuries.
- Always wear a mask during foil drill.
- If you are a woman, wear a breast protector.
- If you are a novice, use a blade that bends easily.
- Wear underarm protectors (plastrons).
- Check equipment carefully before each match and practice session.

- Make sure there are no obstructions at the end and sides of the fencing area.
- Whenever you are not using the foil, carry it handle end down with the blade held close to your arm. You may also rest the foil on the floor with the hilt down, grasping the blade in your hand.
- Always replace a broken blade. Do not try to tape it and continue to use it.

- You must wear adequate protective equipment, including a glove on your weapon hand.
- Learn to put on and take off your mask with only the unarmed hand. If you have to use two hands, put down the foil so that its tip presents no hazard to the eyes of anyone in range.
- Do not begin to fence with others until you have complete control of your blade and body movements. Without complete control, you are a menace to your partner.
- When beginning, learn to attack and defend only the high target area above the waist, which is the area where most touches are made. Inclusion of the low target area would require the fencer to wear trousers and groin protection.
- Because of the heat-retaining characteristics of the canvas jacket and mask, you should moderate drills on hot days and take frequent rests.
- An important safety skill to learn is the judgment of distance. Misjudging distance frequently causes broken blades, which can cause injury.

Rifle Marksmanship

RISK FACTORS

- Although there are no North American data available for injuries or deaths on rifle ranges, an estimated 550 people are accidentally killed annually by firearms.

CONTRIBUTING FACTORS

- lead poisoning
- being struck by a bullet
- failure to wear ear and eye protection

COMMENT

While some hunters put away their rifles at the end of hunting season, many others simply begin a new shooting season on rifle and pistol ranges. Many non-hunters use rifle ranges all year. The record of safe gun handling on target ranges over the years has been exceptionally good; however, there are some safety factors that should continue to be observed to keep the sport safe.

SAFETY SENSE

- Treat every rifle as if it were loaded. Never ask if a gun is loaded. The owner might be wrong. Check it for yourself.
- Be familiar with the handling and workings of your rifle and ammunition.
- Keep the muzzle pointed in a safe direction, always down the range.
- Always keep the breech action open when not shooting. Other people have the right to know that your rifle is safe.
- Keep your finger out of the trigger guard until your sights are on the target.
- Be sure that your backstop is secure and thick enough for the caliber of ammunition used.

- Obey every firing-line command at once.
- Wear hearing protection such as ear plugs or, preferably, ear muffs. Continued exposure to the sound of rifle shots can cause hearing damage.
- It is wise to wear eye protection to be safe from the accidental ejection of a rifle cartridge from your rifle, or someone else's, into your face.
- On ranges that are used excessively for long periods of time, there may be high levels of poisonous lead in the air from bullets. Ensure that your range has proper ventilation, switch ammunition to semi-jacket lead bullets, and encourage the range management to monitor the levels of lead contamination.

Roller-Skating

RISK FACTORS
- Over 80 percent of roller-skaters do not use protective equipment.
- About 75 percent of all injuries occur outside organized skating rinks.
- The parts of the body at greatest risk of injury are the hands, wrists, and elbows.

CONTRIBUTING FACTORS
- failure to wear protective equipment
- loss of balance
- skating too fast
- irregularities in the skating surface

COMMENT

Long considered a pastime of children, roller-skating has been discovered by adults who are enjoying the sensation of flying and the benefits of a good cardio-vascular workout without the harsh pounding of limbs on the pavement. You may envy the grace, agility, and speed of skillful roller-skaters, but the sport is not as easy as it looks. Moving at high speed on small wheels requires not only skill but also quality equipment in good condition.

SAFETY SENSE

- Wear protective clothing, including leather gloves, knee protectors, and a hockey or bicycle safety helmet.
- It is advisable to skate in a roller rink where there are no hills or unexpected bumps and potholes.
- Check your jurisdiction for laws relating to skating on streets and sidewalks. Some localities have banned roller skates from public roads.
- Before starting, warm up your muscles to prevent strains and pulled muscles.
- When you fall, you will minimize injury if you try to relax as you are falling.

Table Tennis

RISK FACTORS
- No North American data are available.

CONTRIBUTING FACTORS
- falling into table corner edges
- being hit in the eye by a ball
- being struck by a paddle
- wearing improper footwear

COMMENT

Table tennis, also known as ping-pong, began in the 1890s. All you need for equipment is a ball, a racquet (paddle/bat), a flat table measuring 2.7 m by 1.5 m (9 ft. by 5 ft.) with the playing surface 75 cm (30 in.) from the floor, and a net with supports. There should be at least 6 m (20 ft.) of open space behind each end of the table to allow safe movement. The majority of injuries associated with the game are minor muscle strains and wrist and arm soreness.

SAFETY SENSE

- Be careful not to spear yourself on a corner of the table.
- If you play competitive table tennis, you must be in good physical condition. Do a 15-minute warm-up of arm, wrist, and hand exercises to help prevent sprains and strained muscles.
- Always wear running shoes. Playing in stocking feet will contribute to slips and falls. You may wear special table tennis shoes, but typical running shoes will suffice.
- Wear sport safety glasses while playing.
- Replace your paddle once it has been damaged or the grip has become smooth.

OUTDOOR RECREATION

North Americans by the millions flock to the woods, oceans, mountains, parks, lakes, and rivers for recreational activities. They get there by foot, car, recreational vehicle, and all-terrain vehicle, in spite of the fact that many of these sites are primitive and inconvenient. Through participating in outdoor activities, they seek fun, enjoyment, education, adventure, and excitement.

Outdoor recreation deals with the use, enjoyment, and understanding of our natural environment. It encompasses interests as diverse as camping, viewing a sunset, and gathering shells on an ocean beach. The desires for adventure, for learning about the natural world, and for appreciating beauty are universal. However, if you want to continue to enjoy all the benefits of outdoor recreation, you should also consider the dangers.

All-Terrain Vehicles (ATVs)

RISK FACTORS

- Children under 16 years of age account for 40 percent of reported injuries and deaths; children under 12 account for 15 percent.
- Ninety percent of ATV-related injuries occur during recreational use.
- Fifty-five percent of all accident victims were not wearing any protective equipment.
- Fifty percent of all accident victims were not wearing safety helmets.
- Twenty percent of all accident victims were passengers.
- Fifteen percent of all drivers in accidents had recently consumed alcohol. Among adult drivers, this percentage is much higher.
- Ten percent of people injured were first-time riders.
- Twenty percent of all accidents occur on public roads.
- ATVs overturn in 70 percent of all accidents.
- In this 70 percent of accidents, 50 percent of ATVs capsize sideways, 30 percent capsize backward, and 20 percent capsize forward.
- Approximately three percent of all ATV accidents are directly attributable to the mechanical condition of the machine.

CONTRIBUTING FACTORS

- vehicle overturned
- excessive speed
- inexperienced operator
- poor knowledge of the capabilities of ATVs
- poor understanding of safety rules, laws, and regulations
- failing to wear a safety helmet
- failing to wear eye, foot, or body protection
- carrying passengers
- travelling on public roads
- hitting fixed objects
- unstable vehicle
- losing control of ATV
- impaired judgment and skill due to alcohol consumption
- underinflated or overinflated tires
- defective controls and lighting system
- fires resulting from gasoline leaks

COMMENT

Four-wheeled ATVs were once used primarily for travelling across rough terrain, such as farms, bush, and wilderness areas. The popularity of recreational trail riding, however, has increased dramatically in the past few years.

ATVs have large, low-pressure tires that provide excellent suspension, enabling them to travel easily over rough terrain, mud, and snow. They have largely replaced snowmobiles, both for work and for recreation.

ATVs are dangerous if not operated carefully, so you should take special care to prevent injury. Knowing all you can about your ATV and about the rules and regulations controlling its use will help you prepare for safe and enjoyable driving. Remember, ATVs are intended for off-highway use, not for use on paved surfaces.

SAFETY SENSE

- Children under 12 years of age should not be allowed to operate an ATV.
- Children under 16 years of age should receive safety instruction and drive only under the supervision of an adult.
- ATVs should only be started and re-fuelled by adults.
- Even though most jurisdictions do not have age restrictions on the use of ATVs, some do prohibit children under the age of 14 from operating on or crossing over public roads.
- Make sure your children possess the necessary mental and physical skills to drive an ATV safely by carefully observing them the first time they ride.
- If you decide to teach your children to use an ATV, you must become familiar with its controls, handling characteristics, maintenance requirements, and proper driving techniques.
- Show your children all the parts of the machine that could cause burns or other injuries.

- To avoid injury, your children's feet must always stay on the footrests while they are riding. Be sure to stress this important rule.
- Always equip your children with the proper protective clothing.
- Never allow your children to carry passengers or to ride as passengers. ATVs are designed only for single riders.
- It is important that your children always ride ATVs of the right size. They should not ride vehicles that require them to stretch to put their feet on the footrests or their hands on the handlebars. Follow the manufacturers' recommendations on size guidelines.
- Your children's safety depends on the mechanical condition of the ATV; be sure to inspect the machine and keep it maintained.
- Select an approved helmet that meets Standard D230 of the Canadian Standards Association, U.S. Federal Motor Vehicle Safety Standard 218, or the standards of the British Standards Institute.

- Your helmet should fit snugly and be fastened securely. A helmet with a full faceplate provides extra protection. Helmets that leave your face unprotected are lighter and cooler, but they should be used with mouth and eye protection.
- Without eye protection, you risk serious injury or even blindness. Regular sunglasses do not provide proper protection. Always use a face shield or goggles.
- Good gloves will offer protection in the event of a spill, as well as preventing your hands from getting sore or cold.
- The best protective footwear is a pair of boots with heels to prevent your feet from slipping off the pegs.
- Protect your skin from scratches with a long-sleeved shirt and long pants. Off-road pants with knee pads or jerseys with elbow and shoulder pads provide even better protection, as well as looking stylish.
- Register your ATV with the appropriate agency.
- Carry liability insurance.
- Do not operate ATVs on public roads. They are designed for off-road use only.
- Cross roads only at right angles. Always stop and yield the right-of-way to other vehicles and pedestrians.
- Report all accidents involving injury, property damage, or death to the police.
- To prevent injury, always keep your feet on the footrests while riding.
- When mounting an ATV, take care not to step on the gear shifter.
- If your ATV starts to tip while turning, reduce your speed, lean your upper body farther into the turn, and make the turn wider.

- Some hills are too steep for your abilities and/or your ATV's capabilities; if you have any doubts about a hill, don't try to climb it.
- Shift your body weight forward when climbing hills to prevent your ATV from flipping over backwards.
- Do not let your ATV roll backward on a hill. If it begins to roll backward, dismount to the side immediately.
- Do not attempt to back down a hill using the rear brake. You may flip over backward.
- Traversing a slope is a tricky maneuvre. Avoid slopes if they are slippery or very bumpy.
- If you must dismount from an ATV on a hill, always dismount on the uphill side of the machine to prevent the possibility of the ATV rolling over on top of you.
- On firm snow you can have fun on your ATV, but do not drive on soft snow. You could easily roll over or get stuck and stranded.
- Do not venture onto frozen lakes or rivers that are unfamiliar.
- Determine the thickness of all ice surfaces before travelling on them.
- Never carry a passenger on an ATV.
- Don't drink and drive. Plan your social activities at the end of the ATV trip.
- Refuse to go riding with any driver who has been drinking.
- Since ATVs are not allowed on public roads, you should ride only on private property. The owners of the property should exercise prudent control over the consumption of alcohol because they are open to a personal liability suit in the case of an accident.
- Always maintain the manufacturers' recommended air pressure in the tires. You will need a low-pressure

air gauge because automotive gauges will not measure the required pressure range.

- Check tires for cuts and gashes that could cause air leakage.
- Losing a tire could cause you to lose control of your vehicle, so check the axle nuts regularly and make sure they are secured by cotter pins.
- Check all wheel lug nuts periodically.
- Make sure the throttle moves smoothly and snaps closed, regardless of what position the handle bars are in.
- Keep all cables free of dirt.
- Have your brakes checked regularly and keep them in excellent condition.

- Ensure that the gearshift pedal is firmly attached to the vehicle and that it is positioned for safe operation.
- Ensure that the lights, emergency stop, and ignition switches are working.
- Check your machine regularly for oil and fuel leaks, especially after use on rough terrain.
- Inspect the drive chain for proper adjustment, adequate lubrication, and wear.
- Driving on rough terrain will loosen parts, so check nuts and bolts before, during, and after use.
- Always start your ride with a full tank of gas in case you get lost.

Archery

RISK FACTORS
- Approximately 4,000 people receive medical attention each year in North America for injuries related to archery.

CONTRIBUTING FACTORS
- improper shooting technique
- lack of proper protection
- poorly selected and maintained equipment
- getting hit by an arrow
- poor range condition
- self-inflicted wounds

COMMENT

People have been shooting arrows for at least 20,000 years. Originally, people used them to hunt for food and clothing. Today, they are used on target ranges, for hunting, and as general recreation. Whether you shoot in your backyard or in the woods, remember that bows and arrows are dangerous; never handle them as if they were toys.

SAFETY SENSE

- Indoor ranges are somewhat safer than outdoor ranges, simply because it is easier for the instructor to supervise the students.
- Access to ranges by non-participants should be controlled. Ranges must have suitable backstops, such as bales of hay or clear areas behind targets.
- Shooting lines must be established for each shooting distance on the range.
- Keep archery equipment in good condition. Equipment failure due to abuse, neglect, and aging are preventable. Arrows may be cracked or splintered; strings may be strung too tightly, strung too loosely or missing.
- Archers should use protective equipment, including shooting tabs or gloves and arm guards.
- Arrows must be long enough that they cannot be overdrawn. An overdrawn arrow can cause an injury.
- Shooting an unarmed bow can break the string or the bow. The flying pieces could injure you or others nearby.
- When shooting on a range, follow the commands of the range supervisor or instructor.

- Never retrieve an arrow from your target while other people are still shooting. Wait until the range shooting time is finished.
- Remove large buttons, pins, watches, bulky sweaters, eye glasses, pens, and pencils before shooting.
- Use bows that are easy to pull until you have learned proper archery techniques and have conditioned your body to control more powerful bows.
- Never cloud shoot (shoot an arrow into the sky). It may hit someone.
- Always shoot at least 450 m (1,500 ft.) from any residence.
- Carry all arrows in a quiver that encloses the head points.
- Never carry a bow that is nocked or loaded. Nock your arrow (fit it to the bowstring) only when it is your turn to shoot.
- Do not carry your bow when climbing; if your hands are not free, you may fall. When hunting from a tree blind or stand, tie a string on the bow and pull it up after you have reached your position. When crossing a fence, lay your bow down then reach back for it.
- When hunting with a partner, know his or her position at all times.
- Many archers suffer from blisters, calluses, or numbness of the fingers. Usually these injuries are a result of improper hand positioning, torque on the string, or shooting too many arrows in a day.
- Lack of conditioning and poor pulling techniques can lead to painful muscle strains. Always warm up your upper body before shooting. Competitive archers condition both sides of their bodies to prevent imbalances.

Camping

RISK FACTORS
• No North American data are available.

CONTRIBUTING FACTORS
• carbon monoxide poisoning
• poisoning from plants or spoiled food
• insect/animal bites
• cuts and burns
• sunburn

COMMENT

More and more families are enjoying the pleasures of camping and outdoor life. Some advance planning will make camping trips both more enjoyable and safer. Make sure that everything you take is in good condition and functioning properly. Test all your equipment before you leave: set up the tent, light the lantern, and test the stove. If you are a novice camper, you may want to take a practice trip nearby before going on a more ambitious adventure.

Look for a campsite that is well-drained, with a good combination of sun and shade. Check the area for hazards, and instruct your children about things to avoid, such as poisonous plants, wild animals, and moving vehicles.

SAFETY SENSE

• Wear shoes, sandals, or moccasins at your campsite; glass, cans, sharp rocks, and hot embers can hurt bare feet.
• If you bring perishable food, use a portable ice chest to keep it from spoiling. If you suspect that food is tainted, throw it out.
• Keep the site clean. Dispose of cans, bottles, and garbage safely in a campground trash can, roadside refuse barrel, or community dump.
• Only drink water from sources that are posted as being safe. If you have any doubts, boil it first or use water purification tablets.
• Obey signs and warnings concerning wildlife. If raccoons, skunks, porcupines, or other small animals come to your campsite, scare them away

with a flashlight or a loud noise. Don't keep food in your tent where it can be smelled by the animals; store it away from the campsite.

- Light wood fires only in authorized areas, preferably downwind from your campsite. Clear away leaves and other combustible material. Avoid loose clothing that leaves your skin exposed to flame and sparks. Keep children away from the fire.
- Never leave a fire unattended. When finished with it, spread the burned pieces, soak them thoroughly with water, and then cover them with sand.
- Never leave fuel or compressed gas containers close to a fire or in a tent.
- Handle fuel-powered lanterns and heaters with care. If possible, use battery-powered equipment.
- Do not cook in your tent.
- Winter camping requires special knowledge on how to keep warm and avoid frostbite. Consult a camping store or library to find out what equipment you will require.
- Before going to a forested area, check the fire hazard index with the park rangers. Help prevent forest fires by watching your smoking habits. Smoke only in designated areas and never while walking.
- Before leaving your campsite to hike or boat, listen to weather reports on the radio.
- Never seek shelter from a lightning storm under a tree; stay in a ditch or a low place and wait until the storm is over.

Cycling

RISK FACTORS

- Fifty percent of all bicycle injuries result from falls.
- Over 80 percent of all bicycle fatalities involve another vehicle.
- Over 70 percent of all collisions between bicycles and motor vehicles occur at intersections and driveways.
- Sixty-six percent of bicyclists killed or seriously injured in collisions with automobiles have violated a law or safety rule.

CONTRIBUTING FACTORS

- streetcar and railway tracks
- weather hazards
- dangerous road surfaces
- making improper turns
- failing to yield the right of way
- failing to wear a suitable helmet
- failing to maintain the bicycle in good mechanical order
- an ill-fitting bicycle
- using infant carriers on the back of the bicycle
- inadequate lighting on the bicycle
- failing to use reflective material on clothing
- poor knowledge and observance of traffic rules and regulations
- failing to stop at all signed intersections
- poor brakes
- inability to keep the bicycle balanced properly

COMMENT

Some people consider bicycles to be toys, while others use them for transportation and exercise. Either way, a bicycle can be dangerous if the rider does not use safety sense. Most motor vehicle drivers in North America do not have enough consideration for cyclists. But even the most careful driver may not see a cyclist who is not equipped with proper reflective clothing, and reflectors and a headlamp on the bicycle. Cyclists must protect themselves by anticipating discourteous and irresponsible drivers. They must also obey the rules of the road.

- Cross all streetcar and railway tracks at an angle between 45 and 90 degrees to avoid getting your tires caught in the tracks.
- Approach all holes and depressions cautiously. Go around them gradually or through them slowly.
- Go over loose or slippery surfaces slowly. Turn corners carefully, keeping your bicycle as upright as possible.
- Raised surfaces can buckle your wheels and throw you out of control. Look out for raised manhole covers, tracks, and stones.
- Riding over sharp objects can cut or puncture your tires. This can cause blowouts, which often result in spills or crashes.
- Most cities and towns forbid riding on sidewalks unless the wheel diameter is no more than 60 cm (20 in.).
- Most bicycle brakes work poorly in the rain. If you have steel rims, ride more slowly and brake sooner when it is raining. Aluminum rims provide the best braking in wet weather.
- Overnight freezes can leave patches of frost and black ice on the road. Use only the back brake (not the front one) when slowing down. If your front brake locks up, you will lose steering control.
- Riding in cold weather causes rapid heat loss in your extremities, so dress warmly.
- Watch for cars approaching from the opposite direction that may turn left in front of you. Motorists often do not look out for cyclists.
- Avoid putting yourself in a position where cars can cut you off. Stay on the right edge of the traffic flow, but keep safely away from the curb.
- Stay at least a door's width away when passing parked cars.
- Establish eye contact with motorists at intersections. Be especially careful with drivers on the right, who may pull out in front of you.
- Avoid getting stuck on the wrong side of a turning vehicle or being in the right-turn-only lane when you plan to ride straight through.
- Always yield the right of way if you find yourself in a potentially dangerous situation.
- Be thoroughly familiar with all the operating controls on your bicycle; their use should become second nature to you.
- Ensure that your brake handles are securely fastened to your handle bars.
- Make sure your wheels are straight and tightly mounted. The rims should be free of dents, which will affect braking.
- Your clothing should not flap in the wind as you ride. Secure your pant legs by using bicycle clips or tucking them into your socks so they do not catch in the chain.
- Shoes should have stiff inner soles for maximum comfort. The soles should be corrugated to prevent slipping, unless you have toe clips.
- Do not use an infant carrier.
- If you use a generated light (one that is attached to the bicycle wheel), remember that it will go out when you stop.
- Riding at dawn and dusk is especially dangerous because everyone's eyes have difficulty adjusting to rapidly changing light levels.
- White reflective tape on the front forks and red reflective tape on the stays attached to the rear wheel will make you more visible from the side. Pedal reflectors provide additional visibility.
- Bright, reflective clothing is best for riding both at night and during the day. A white or yellow helmet with reflective material on it is also highly visible.

- Reflective wrist bands make your hand signals more visible.
- Bands of reflective material on your ankles or your shoe heels help to make you more visible.
- Bicycles are subject to the same traffic rules as vehicular traffic, so obey all street signs and regulations.
- Ride on the right-hand side of the road with traffic, not against it.
- Ride single file.
- Hitching a ride on a moving vehicle is illegal and dangerous.
- Use arm signals to indicate that you intend to stop or turn.
- Do not carry packages that interfere with your vision or control.
- Bicyclists are prohibited from riding on expressways, freeways, and roads that have "no bicycle" signs posted.
- Bicycles must yield to pedestrians.
- Lights are required for nighttime riding.
- A bicycle must have a horn or bell in case you have to sound a warning.
- Use a bicycle that fits your size, build, and style of riding. Do not allow young children to ride bicycles that are too large for them to operate safely.
- Get the salesperson to help adjust the bicycle before you buy it.
- Before purchasing a bicycle, ride it around the block to determine if the saddle is comfortable.
- Ensure that the bicycle steers straight when your hands are off the handlebars. Do not do this in traffic.

Hiking

RISK FACTORS
- No North American data are available.

CONTRIBUTING FACTORS
- improperly fitting boots, wrinkled socks, and excessive moisture in boots
- drowning
- insect/animal bites
- dehydration
- sprains and strains
- sunburn
- frostbite and snowblindness
- slips and falls
- getting lost in the woods

COMMENT

Hiking refers to extended walks, primarily in rural areas on unpaved surfaces, such as paths, abandoned railway lines, and country pastures. Hiking generally involves only day trips. Back packing for overnight trips requires equipment, food, and shelter.

SAFETY SENSE

- Do not wear cotton clothing in cold weather. It retains moisture, allowing your body to lose heat easily.
- Dress in layers. The inner layer should be polypropylene underwear. Good outer layers are a wool or pile jacket topped with a jacket and pants that will break the wind. Avoid coated nylon clothing.
- Carry at least one litre (0.25 gals.) of water and more if it is really hot.
- Take along high-calorie snacks and lunches, such as nuts, cheese, dried fruit, and peanut butter.
- Always take rain gear with you.

- Wear a toque in cooler weather to prevent heat loss from your head.
- Wear two pairs of socks -- thin polypropylene ones next to the skin and thick wool ones over those.
- Do not wear running shoes. They offer no ankle support. Purchase lightweight hiking boots instead. They should be well-fitted, with good treads and a rockered heel that will align the foot with the leg when it hits the ground. Waterproof your boots.
- Wear cross-country skiing gaiters (ankle protectors) in sloppy conditions to keep mud out of your boots.

- Keep a change of clothes, including dry shoes, in your vehicle. Driving home wet is no fun.
- Take emergency hiking gear with you on overnight trips. Include a water filter, plastic cups and dishes, leakproof water and food containers, a Swiss army knife, water-purifying tablets, a fuel bottle, a gas stove, and a sleeping bag.
- Remember, the return trip is just as far as the trip in. Do not overextend yourself.
- To prevent eye soreness, even in the winter, use sunglasses on sunny days.
- Wear a helmet when hiking in rough terrain with loose rocks or steep inclines.
- In the woods, you risk being hit by falling dead trees or branches. You may also slip and fall on a tree branch. Be careful when climbing over trees, especially if they are wet or rotten.

- When day hiking, leave information with family members or neighbors on the general area in which you plan to hike.
- Rest often during a hike.
- Be aware that if you hold branches for the hiker behind you, they may snap back and cause an injury.
- Always keep an eye out for animals. Be particularly careful if there has been a recent rabies outbreak in your area.
- Do not hike on active railway property or cross over rivers on a train bridge. Remember, anytime is train time.
- If using a roadway, hike on the left side facing oncoming vehicles.
- If you get lost, stay where you are. Searchers will begin looking for you where you were last seen. See Specialty Topics, page 216 for how to protect yourself if you become lost.

Horse Racing

- No North American data are available. However, one study estimated that more than 110 jockeys have died from racing accidents since World War II.

CONTRIBUTING FACTORS
- position of the jockey on the mount
- collisions between horses
- horses that trip or get injured
- failing to hurdle a jump in a steeplechase race
- poor track condition

COMMENT

Horse racing is known as the sport of kings. For 3,000 years, from chariot-loving Assyrian monarchs down to the present British queen, Elizabeth II, royalty have been the leading owners of racing stables. Jockeys (riders) are professionals who seldom weigh more than 52 kg (115 lbs.). This sport demands that jockeys be superior athletes prepared to face the risk of serious injury. The position in which jockeys ride their mounts contributes to serious injury. A jockey does not sit on a horse, but rather grips it with the knees and thighs while leaning forward. The jockey's back is parallel to that of the horse. If the horse stops suddenly, the jockey is propelled forward, possibly into the path of other horses. Head, neck, and spine injuries can result.

SAFETY SENSE

- A physician should always be present during a race, and an ambulance with paramedics should follow the horses around the track, ready to provide immediate medical attention to an injured jockey.
- Any jockey involved in an accident must be examined by a doctor before his or her next race.
- Jockeys must wear protective helmets. They should also wear shoulder pads and padded vests, such as those used in steeplechase races.
- The railing around the race track should be able to withstand the impact of a horse without breaking loose or shattering. The railing should be offset from the upright posts so that a jockey thrown to the track can roll under it, away from the horses' hooves. The railing should

not have any protruding objects that could stab a jockey who lands on it.

- Jockeys lead stressful lives. They may ride four or five mounts in nine races. They may ride in the morning in Toronto and in the evening in New York City. This stress leads to poor physical conditioning, which increases the chances of muscle strain, fatigue, and injuries.

- Weight and diet control is essential for a jockey. Poor dietary habits can lead to fainting and falling off a mount during a race.

Horseback Riding

RISK FACTORS
- Approximately 52,000 North Americans each year are treated for injuries resulting from accidents involving horseback riding.
- In one study, falling from a horse accounted for 66 percent of the reported riding accidents.
- One study states that 33 percent of horseback riding-related deaths resulted from head injuries.

CONTRIBUTING FACTORS
- falling off the horse
- the horse falling
- being kicked or stepped on by the horse
- poor horsemanship
- failing to wear protective head gear

COMMENT

Millions of people in North America ride horses. Many enjoy slow-paced, peaceful afternoon riding through woods; others ride at a club; others make a living using horses on farms and ranches; still others enter horseback-riding competitions. Whatever the reason for riding, a certain amount of risk is involved, yet many injuries could be avoided by taking a few precautions.

SAFETY SENSE

- Knowing your horse's ability and your own ability as a rider will minimize riding risks.
- A major danger of horseback riding is falling from the horse, which may result in a head injury. A protective helmet is the most important piece of equipment you can use. It is important that your helmet or hat fit snugly and be able to resist penetration. It should have a chin strap to ensure that it remains securely on your head. The peak, if it has one, should be flexible.

- Wear proper footwear. Do not go barefoot or wear running shoes. Raised heels are essential.
- Riding clothing should be comfortable and fit properly. Loose-fitting, flapping clothing may scare the horse, making it jump unexpectedly. Wear long pants; skin burns from rubbing against the saddle can really hurt.
- If you own your own equipment, keep it in good condition. A worn bridle or weakened cinch could cause a serious accident. Make sure

the cinch (the strap that holds the saddle on) is properly tightened and checked frequently.

- If you are a beginner, take riding lessons. Good instruction not only teaches the rider the necessary skills, but it teaches horsemanship. Understanding what makes a horse stop, start, shy, kick, and balk can help prevent an accident.
- If you are renting a horse, tell the management what your true riding ability is so they can match a horse to your level of skill.
- Always keep the ball of your foot on the stirrup. Do not put your foot through to the boot heel. This way, if your horse spooks your feet will come out of the stirrups easily.
- Approach a horse from the front left side if possible. Talk to the horse, letting it know you are coming near.
- Almost all horses like to move around while being mounted. They are usually anxious to get going. Be sure that the horse doesn't step on your foot.
- Never mount a horse inside a barn. A horse could side-step and crush you against something, or you could hit your head on an overhanging object.
- When following another horse on a path, keep your horse well back. Horses can become jealous and may kick at the horse behind.
- Walk, don't ride, your horse through dangerous areas, such as thick bush, steep hills, and rocky terrain.
- If possible, stay away from hard surfaces, such as pavement, cement, and rock areas. These surfaces increase the chance of the horse slipping and falling.
- Be aware of overhanging branches and ground obstructions, such as holes or tree roots. Never hold back a branch for the person following you. If it slips, it could cause an injury.

Horseshoe Pitching

RISK FACTORS
- Approximately 3,000 people in North America are treated each year for injuries received while horseshoe pitching.

CONTRIBUTING FACTORS
- being hit by a horseshoe
- muscle strain

COMMENT

Horseshoe pitching probably started with idle Roman officers who played quoits during the occupation of Britain from the first to fifth centuries. In the game of quoits, one of five games in the ancient Greek pentathlon, players throw metal, rubber, or rope rings around pegs. Romans may have used horseshoes when they didn't have quoits.

The game of horseshoes is played on a regulation court, or anywhere two stakes can be placed at least 9.14 m (30 ft.) apart for women and 12.19 m (40 ft.) apart for men. Whether in backyard pits or city parks, horseshoe pitching is a low-key competitive pastime. It is an economical way to enjoy the outdoors, get a little exercise, and spend time with friends.

SAFETY SENSE

- Wear recreational steel-toed shoes. A 1 kg (2.2 lbs.) horseshoe can break a bone in your foot very easily.
- Stretch and warm up your upper body before each game to prevent muscle soreness in your shoulders and arms.
- When not pitching, stay well back and to the side of your opponents.

Horseshoes can slip out of a thrower's hand and hit the player standing behind. Wear a sand hand rub (special type of glove) to give you a firm grip on the horseshoe.
- Join a horseshoe-pitching club and learn the proper throwing techniques. This will prevent injuries due to pulled muscles.

RISK FACTORS
- Approximately 550 deaths annually in North America result from firearm accidents in public places. Some are the result of hunting accidents.
- Accidentally self-inflicted wounds account for about 30 percent of hunting accidents.
- More accidents occur during deer-hunting season than any other time.

CONTRIBUTING FACTORS
- the victim moving into the line of fire
- the victim being mistaken for game
- slipping and falling
- discharging a firearm accidentally when removing it from a vehicle, when crossing obstacles, or while riding on or in a vehicle
- a stray bullet ricocheting
- recklessness and horseplay

COMMENT

Pilots are often told, "When you enter the cockpit of an aircraft, you become part of a system over which you have control, both in terms of operation and safe handling. You are the only one that can make the system safe or unsafe." The same advice applies to hunters. From the time you pick up a firearm, you become a part of a system over which you have complete control. You are the only part of the system that can make a gun or rifle safe or unsafe.

SAFETY SENSE

- Treat every gun or rifle as if it were loaded and ready to fire.
- Always point the muzzle in a safe direction.
- Be sure of your target and of what is beyond it.
- Do not carry deer skins or antlers in such a way that you could be mistaken for a deer.
- Wear bright, reflective clothing, so you stand out to other hunters. Blaze orange is an effective color.
- Among other things, protecting yourself requires getting over, through, and around obstacles. Do it carefully, ensuring that your weapon is unloaded first. If it is loaded, place the weapon flat on the ground, then reach back for it. If hunting in pairs, one hunter can hold both weapons then pass them over when the second hunter has crossed the obstacle.

- If the weapon is loaded, leave the safety catch on. Keep your fingers outside the trigger guard except when ready to shoot.
- There are many ways to carry a weapon safely, depending on who is around you. Carrying it with the barrel over your shoulder is safe unless someone is behind you. Carrying it cradled in the bend of your elbow is safe unless someone is in front of you. Carrying it facing to the side is safe unless someone is on that side. As a hunter, you should know where your companions are at all times.
- In group hunting, set some safety ground rules before the hunt begins. Determine such issues as who will scare up the birds, who will get to shoot, and where you will meet.
- In most jurisdictions, hunters must show proof of having taken a hunter safety course in order to obtain a hunting permit. If you are planning to start hunting, take a safety course even if it is not required to qualify for a license.

Jogging

RISK FACTORS
- Thirteen percent of all pedestrian jogging accidents occur on roadways.

CONTRIBUTION FACTORS
- listening to a radio headset while jogging
- failing to wear reflective clothing while jogging at night or in stormy weather
- jogging on the right side of the road instead of on the left side, facing oncoming traffic
- insufficient warm-up exercises

COMMENT

Millions of people jog seriously. What might have started as a casual romance is now a very serious affair for many. You should not simply hit the streets for your exercise, however. There are some safety sense precautions that you should observe.

SAFETY SENSE

- When jogging at night on public roads, be sure to wear light-colored reflective or retroreflective clothing. Better yet, reschedule your runs to daylight hours.
- Do not jog at night in strange cities or neighborhoods unless you are certain that it is safe to do so.
- Jogging on main city streets, particularly when traffic is heavy, is harmful due to the polluted air from vehicle exhaust systems.
- Where possible, jog in parks and fields instead of on roads and sidewalks.
- Make sure your running shoes have enough tread to grip slippery surfaces, especially during the winter. If it is icy outside, take the day off from jogging.
- Muscles are especially susceptible to strains in the cold. During winter, stretch indoors before and after your run.
- Be considerate of slower-moving pedestrians when jogging on the sidewalk.
- Joggers must obey all traffic controls and rules of the road.

- Running until you are exhausted is dangerous and may cause long-term injury.
- Do not jog on a public street while using a radio headset.
- The inability to keep your body temperature from rising too high or dropping too low during a run can result in serious harm. Select proper clothing for the weather conditions.

Wear white cotton clothing in hot weather, rather than nylon fabrics. Winter jogging demands that you wear lightweight clothing designed to keep you warm. Cover your head and hands to prevent heat loss and frostbite.
- Drink fluids (mainly cool water) before and after you run to reduce dehydration.

Motorcycle Trail Riding

RISK FACTORS

- It is estimated that over 25,000 people receive medical attention each year in North America from trail bike accidents.

CONTRIBUTING FACTORS

- unfamiliarity with the trail
- failing to wear protective equipment
- losing control of the vehicle
- inexperienced riders
- riding too fast for trail conditions

COMMENT

Trail riding, or dirt riding, requires different skills and techniques than regular road riding. Trail bikes have a different tire tread design and their engines supply more power at low speeds for hill climbing. They are lighter weight, with heavy-duty suspension systems and wider handle bars for greater steering leverage. As in all sports, experience plays a major role in reducing accidents. Begin gradually on gentle terrain before attempting more difficult trails. And, before attempting a challenging trail ride, travel your intended course slowly at first. New hazards, such as fallen trees, may show up overnight.

SAFETY SENSE

- Check weather conditions before a ride.
- Obtain permission before riding on private property.
- Avoid riding in areas that could be damaged by your vehicle, such as soft meadows, freshly seeded areas, and steep hillsides where erosion might occur.
- Respect signs, fences, and gates. Respect animal life, both wild and domestic.
- When riding in forests or dry fields, be sure a spark arrester is attached to the exhaust system.
- Stay out of restricted places, such as slide areas, watersheds, or high-risk fire areas. Avoid horse trails -- horses frighten easily.
- Carry a tool box for emergency repairs.
- Wear protective clothing -- a helmet, sturdy footwear, eye protection, gloves, and a jacket.

Motorcycling

RISK FACTORS

- More than 50 percent of all motorcycle fatalities involve drivers under 25 years of age.
- Losing control of the motorcycle accounts for about 10 percent of all fatalities.
- About 40 percent of the motorcycle riders in fatal accidents had been drinking.
- In jurisdictions lacking helmet laws, there are two to three times the number of serious head injuries per registered motorcycle.
- Over 50 percent of fatal crashes involve collisions with other vehicles.
- Almost 40 percent of motorcycle accidents involving another vehicle occur at intersections.
- Automobile drivers are at fault in nearly 70 percent of accidents at intersections.
- Speeding is the most common traffic violation.
- Most accidents in which a motorcycle runs off the road without being forced off by another vehicle involve speeding.
- Twenty-five percent of motorcycle accidents involve drivers who have less than six months of riding experience.

CONTRIBUTING FACTORS

- inattentiveness of the motorcyclist
- failing to yield the right-of-way, by either the motorist or the motorcyclist
- limited visibility at intersections
- slippery, loose, or rough surfaces
- railway tracks
- driving at night
- impaired driving due to alcohol consumption
- carrying passengers
- failing to wear a helmet or eye and face protection
- wearing improper footwear
- failing to wear suitable gloves, jacket, and pants
- insufficient time to stop or turn
- failing to slow down for adverse road or weather conditions
- poor motorcycling skills
- insufficient knowledge about the safe use of motorcycles
- lack of motorcycling experience

COMMENT

Millions of people of all ages and from every class of society ride motorcycles on the roads, highways, and streets. Unfortunately, many of those riders will suffer injuries or death from accidents involving their motorcycles.

Motorcycles are one of the most dangerous forms of transportation. Everyone who rides one should exercise safety sense. Most motorcycle accident fatalities result from head injuries. In some jurisdictions, the law requires that riders and passengers on motorcycles wear helmets. Even if the law does not demand that you wear a helmet, you add to your danger of serious injury every time you get on a motorcycle without one.

SAFETY SENSE

- Do not change direction abruptly.
- Always cross railway tracks at an angle between 45 and 90 degrees to prevent the wheels from getting caught in the tracks.
- Be ready to use your feet and body to maintain balance when riding over rough surfaces.
- Be aware of other vehicles and how close they are.
- Use your high-beam headlight as much as possible at night.
- Reduce your speed significantly at night and keep your headlights on.
- Wear a reflective vest at night; other drivers will see it before they notice your taillights.
- Be extremely cautious at the start of a rain shower. The first drops to fall mix with dirt and oil on the road and cut traction dramatically.
- Do not drink if you are going to drive.
- Driving between midnight and three a.m. on weekends is especially dangerous. The bars close, house parties end, and drinking drivers head for home.
- Refuse to ride with any driver who has been drinking.
- Drunk passengers can be as dangerous as drunk drivers. They may fall asleep, lose their balance, or cause the driver to lose control.

- Do not ride with sandals, sneakers, or bare feet.
- Your eye and face protection should permit the use of glasses and sunglasses. It should also allow air to circulate and prevent fogging.
- Wear gloves that fit snugly but are not too tight. Gloves with seamless palms will help prevent blisters, especially on long trips.
- Use only an approved helmet. Make sure it meets the standards of the Snell Memorial Foundation, U.S. Federal Motor Vehicle Safety Standard 218, the British Standards Institute, or the Canadian Standards Association.
- Your helmet must fit your head snugly and comfortably. It must have at least one strong strap that fastens securely under your chin.
- Your helmet should be a bright color, such as white, yellow, or orange. Whether it is or not, put reflective tape on the sides and back to increase your visibility to other motorists.
- Always be prepared to yield the right of way at intersections.
- Slow down when approaching an intersection to give yourself an added margin of safety.
- Be visible. Make sure your headlight is on and wear bright, reflective clothing and equipment.

- Select a lane position that makes it easy for others to see you. It is a good policy to ride in the left half of the traffic lane.
- Leave at least two seconds of distance between your motorcycle and the vehicle ahead. This will assist in preventing a rear-end collision if the vehicle in front stops quickly at an intersection.
- Signal your intentions to other motorists.
- Use the horn if you need to get the attention of other road users.
- Develop a scanning procedure. Look 12 seconds ahead; check left, right, and behind; and keep your eyes moving.
- Be especially cautious at intersections where your range of vision will be limited or where there are residential driveways.
- Watch carefully in intersections for oil and debris, such as car parts, rocks, and garbage.
- Alcohol or drugs and fast driving form a dangerous combination.
- Slow down to a safer speed before entering or turning a corner, especially in adverse conditions.
- When you lean into a curve, your motorcycle and your body should be at the same angle. Do not lean too far. Be sure to warn passengers about this.
- As your speed increases, so must the distance between you and the vehicle in front of you.
- Drive more slowly at night than you would during the day.
- Rapid braking is generally a better and safer way to escape emergencies than increasing speed.
- If you do use the quick acceleration of your bike to get out of a dangerous situation, make sure you have a place to go.
- Enroll in a training course that teaches theory in the classroom, but where you will spend the majority of your time riding your motorcycle. Successfully complete the course before taking the test for your license.
- If you live in an area where people don't ride all year round, practice your skills away from traffic after getting your motorcycle out of winter storage.
- If you buy a new motorcycle, familiarize yourself with it well before riding in traffic.
- Different motorcycles are designed for different types of riding. Know the limitations and characteristics of each type of motorcycle you use.

Mountain Climbing

RISK FACTORS
- No North American data are available. However, in a 10-year study of climbing accidents, 74 percent of all climbers reported reaching their goals without injury. An injury rate of two accidents per 1,000 climbers per year was reported; an average of two climbers per year were killed.

CONTRIBUTING FACTORS
- falling
- slipping while travelling on snow
- gripping loose rock
- getting stranded
- faulty equipment
- failing to use protective equipment
- environmental dangers, such as avalanches and lightning
- inexperience

COMMENT

Mountain climbing is actually one aspect of mountaineering. People who live for years in the mountains learn how to move safely through and over them. These people are mountaineers. When mountaineers use their knowledge and skill to try to climb a particular summit, they become mountain climbers. Today, mountain climbing is a popular sport worldwide.

SAFETY SENSE

- Never engage in horseplay while climbing. The sport is dangerous enough already.
- Be extremely careful not to dislodge stones or rocks that may fall on the climbers following you. If you do, sound a warning. To avoid falling rocks, try not to climb directly behind another climber.
- Do not begin a climb unless you are prepared mentally and physically. Many rescues have been done just to recover a scared climber.
- Do not climb beyond your strength.
- Test all handholds and footholds and watch for spots covered with snow, ice, or water.
- On bare face rock, angles can be deceptive. If they are too steep, they are very dangerous.
- Before standing on the edge of any cliff or ledge, make sure the supporting rock or soil has not been cut away by erosion.
- Start the climb down in time to reach the bottom before dark.
- If a bad storm arises, try to find shelter. Conserve your strength as much as possible by not battling the elements. During an electrical storm, stay away from tall objects such as trees.

- Study your route carefully. Too often, inexperienced climbers stray off course and end up in trouble.
- Before you start climbing, ensure that you have all the necessary climbing equipment, including an ice pick, bilayer (a device for ropes to slide through), rope, and anchors.
- When crossing snowy areas, watch for crevasses.
- Always check in at a park or ranger's station to find out about climbing conditions and safe routes.
- Inexperienced climbers have many accidents. You may have mastered local routes, but when taking on more challenging or unfamiliar routes, be sure you are well prepared.

Orienteering

RISK FACTORS
- No North American data are available.

CONTRIBUTING FACTORS
- sprains and strains
- slipping and falling
- sunburns
- snowblindness and frostbite
- insect/animal bites
- poisonous plants
- improperly fitted footwear
- getting lost in the woods
- drowning

COMMENT

You are standing in a redwood forest, compass in hand. Your objective is to locate an object a kilometre (mile) away. Sorry, there is no trail. You peer at your topographical map and consider the alternatives. Should you climb through the underbrush facing you or trudge up that steep hill? It is your decision. You are orienteering. This is a thinking sport -- the skill of navigating through an unknown area using a map and compass. It is physical exercise with a mental challenge. Hundreds of thousands of people worldwide enjoy this sport. Instruments in hand, they find predesignated points in national and local forests, public lands, and parks.

Orienteering clubs select areas with distinct boundaries so that if someone gets lost or hurt themselves, they can be found easily. A definite finishing time is established and, if participants do not return in time, a search party is sent out to find them.

SAFETY SENSE

- Learn the basic orienteering skills: reading a map and using a compass.
- Carry the basic equipment with you: a compass, the contour map that is handed out at the starting point, appropriate clothing for the season and day, orienteering shoes with cleats or sturdy hiking boots, and sufficient water [at least 1 litre (0.25 gals.)] in hot weather.
- Join a club to learn proper outdoor survival techniques. If you want to try orienteering on your own, then refer to page 216 for safety sense tips on how to survive when lost in the woods before you go on your first trip.
- To avoid getting lost, use the control point or starting point as your point of orientation. Do not always choose the direct route: it may be hazardous.
- Monitor your energy. If you get tired, rest. Fatigue can lead to accidents.
- Refer to additional safety sense tips in the section on Hiking on page 63.

Recreational Trailering

RISK FACTORS

- Recreational trailers are involved in nearly 84 percent of all recreational vehicle accidents.
- Pulling recreational trailers involves the highest risk of accident; driving a self-powered recreational vehicle involves the lowest risk.

CONTRIBUTING FACTORS

- gusts of wind when passing another vehicle
- colliding with a fixed object
- dangerous weather conditions, such as rain, ice, and snow
- difficult road conditions, including slippery, narrow, and rural roads
- improper loading
- defective hitches
- tire or steering failures
- poor driving, due to alcohol impairment or fatigue

COMMENT

Thousands of families join the ranks of trailer enthusiasts every year so they can see the country without leaving the comforts of home. However, a technical problem can throw a wrench into any plans. An engine can overheat if the vehicle is overloaded or travelling at excessive speeds; poor tires can cause an accident. A trailer that is too big for the car can cause the engine to overheat and put a strain on the transmission, brakes, and steering. Because trailers and towing vehicles come in many different weights and sizes, it is important to be as accurate as possible when assessing your equipment needs. Be sure to check the manufacturer's recommendations before selecting a vehicle to tow your trailer.

SAFETY SENSE

- The trailer must be properly wired to the car so that its lights will work.
- The brakes of both the towing vehicle and, if applicable, the trailer should be checked before starting out.
- The towing vehicle, particularly its cooling system and transmission, must be in good mechanical shape before starting out on a trip.
- The heavier the trailer, the longer it takes to stop, so plan your movements well in advance.
- All trailers, especially those weighing over 450 kg (1,000 lbs.), should have brakes.
- Avoid moving the towing vehicle suddenly, as the weight of the trailer could force it to go out of control.
- Check your tire pressure frequently, maintaining correct pressure at all times.
- Avoid slopes, hills, and soft ground when parking a car towing a trailer. If you must park under these conditions, block both the front and back trailer wheels.
- Keep canned goods and other heavy objects on or near the floor of the trailer, thereby maintaining a low center of gravity.
- Do not drive a vehicle that is pulling a trailer when you are tired.
- Keep to the center of the lane when following curves; stay away from the shoulder.
- Use the correct type of hitch for pulling your trailer. If you are in doubt, consult a firm specializing in trailer hitches. Two common types are the ball-frame dead-weight hitch and the axle-mounted hitch.
- Slow down before descending a hill. Prolonged application of the brakes on downgrades causes heat build-up and brake fade.
- Carry emergency equipment, such as a spare tire for the trailer, flares, and tools, at all times.
- Practice turning, stopping, and backing up in an area away from traffic before starting on a trip.

Recreational Vehicles (RVs)

RISK FACTORS

- In one U.S. study, self-powered recreational vehicles (RVs) constituted more than half of the total RV volume on the road, but were involved in only 18 percent of the recorded RV accidents.

CONTRIBUTING FACTORS

- gusts of wind when passing another vehicle
- colliding with fixed objects, such as ditches and rocks
- environmental conditions, such as rain, darkness, and snow
- difficult road conditions including narrow, rural, and mountainous roads
- mechanical defects, particularly in the steering, brakes, or tires
- poor driving, due to alcohol impairment or fatigue

COMMENT

Recreational vehicles (RVs) provide a good way to travel and see the world. They are normally thought of as motor vehicles with built-in cooking and accommodation facilities, but RVs also include trailers pulled by a motor vehicle, full size or mini vans converted into homes on wheels, pickup campers, and converted buses. For tips on the safety sense of travelling with a trailer, refer to page 82.

SAFETY SENSE

- Keep all the vehicle's wheel brakes adjusted to the manufacturer's recommendations.
- Slow down in adverse weather conditions, and do not exceed the mechanical ability of your vehicle.
- Look well ahead when driving to avoid the need for sudden braking. Slow down and stop gradually to prevent needless wear on the braking system.
- Remember that the stopping distance of a vehicle is affected by the condition of its tires, its braking efficiency, its speed, its weight, and the road surface.
- Avoid driving when you are tired. Fatigue can be induced by overeating, drinking alcohol, intense physical exertion, taking drugs, overheating inside the cab of the vehicle, or carbon monoxide. Make sure you are well-rested when starting a trip.
- When you are too drowsy to drive safely, stop and rest.

- Keep your eyes moving. Fixing your eyes on the road can result in highway hypnosis and inattentiveness.
- To relieve tension while driving, do a few neck and shoulder rolls when you are stopped at a traffic light. Or, stop at a rest area and do some light stretching exercises.
- Don't drink and drive.
- Know what the effects of any medication you are taking will be on your driving ability.
- Always maintain at least a four-second distance behind the vehicle in front of you. Scan the roadway well ahead for situations that may suddenly slow traffic.
- Because you have a responsibility to the driver behind your RV, signal all turns well in advance, position your vehicle in the lane according to your intended direction of travel, slow down to encourage tailgaters to pass you by slowing down, and ensure that all your lights are working properly.
- To defend against a head-on crash, constantly scan the road ahead for vehicles or hazards that may force another vehicle into your lane. If a vehicle does come into your lane, move as far to the right as possible and reduce your speed. If necessary, drive onto the shoulder. Drive with your headlights on at all times.
- To avoid accidents at intersections, always know exactly where you want to turn, be aware that other drivers may do something unexpected, and know the rules regarding right of way. Show your intention to turn well in advance, slow your vehicle, and turn without hesitation to avoid confusing other motorists.
- When another vehicle wants to pass, cooperate by staying well within your lane, slowing down, and allowing enough room for the vehicle to return to the lane safely. Blinking your headlights is a courtesy to let passing vehicles know they have cleared your RV and can re-enter the lane.
- Generally, you have nothing to be gained by passing another vehicle going in the same direction unless it is seriously curtailing traffic flow. Before you pass another vehicle, ask yourself if it is necessary. Remember that RVs need extra room to pass, so make sure there are no cars in sight and that you have a long, straight stretch ahead of you.
- RVs have blind spots in which small vehicles go unnoticed. Thoroughly check your blind spot areas before changing lanes or making turns at intersections.
- Because of the hazards of driving in reverse, avoid backing up. Plan your route in advance to eliminate backing up wherever possible.
- Never back around a corner. If you miss a turn, drive around the block. Do not back out of driveways or alleys unless it is unavoidable.
- If you must back up, get out of the vehicle to see how much room you have and what obstacles you must avoid. Clear any movable obstacles out of the way. Then back up slowly, checking both sides. Use a reliable guide to help you maneuvre safely.
- Prepare your vehicle for winter driving, which may include rain, fog, or snow. In case you get stranded, take along extra emergency equipment, such as winter survival clothes and an emergency ration kit.
- If stranded, avoid overexertion and overexposure.
- Make sure you can see by keeping all windows thoroughly clean.
- Keep on hand an adequate supply of windshield wiper fluid.
- Know how to get going in the snow. Remember to use a light touch on the accelerator.
- Learn how to steer in a skid, and remember that excessive speed and hard braking cause most skids.

- Know how to stop in winter conditions. Avoid jamming on the brakes; try steering around the danger if possible.
- Make sure someone knows your planned route and estimated arrival times, especially if you are travelling in isolated areas.
- Listen to weather forecasts prior to and during the trip.
- Reduce speed on rough roads, especially those with sharp-edged potholes.
- Avoid sudden stops.
- Accelerate slowly so you don't spin your wheels.
- Avoid driving on the edge of the pavement.
- Keep your tires properly inflated to manufacturers' recommendations. Underinflation reduces traction and steering control, causes the tire to build up internal heat and pressure, and, in some instances, will cause a wheel fire. Overinflation can cause stress on rims and will create a harder ride. Use a pressure gauge to check all tires. Kicking your tires may make you feel good, but it won't properly measure their pressure.
- Check your tires for cuts and wear. Remove any foreign objects from the treads daily.

Skateboarding

RISK FACTORS
- Forty percent of injuries involve people using borrowed skateboards.
- Fractured arms, wrists, and hands account for 40 percent of all injuries.
- Sprains and strains account for 11 percent of all injuries.

CONTRIBUTING FACTORS
- striking an irregularity in the riding surface
- losing balance
- the skateboard slipping out from under the rider
- tripping over a curb
- riding near traffic

COMMENT

Over the past 15 years, skateboarding has gone through three waves of popularity. (The current wave started around 1985.) Over that same time, three distinct styles of skateboarding have emerged. Ramp-and-pool style is used on specially-made ramps in empty swimming pools. Freestyle involves feats of balance and strength, such as standing on the board while it is on its side or corners and then manipulating it with your feet. Street-style skateboarding tests the skater's ability to go over curbs, ledges, small ramps, and other obstructions commonly encountered on streets and sidewalks. Street-style is probably the most dangerous type of skateboarding, because the rider is exposed to other traffic.

SAFETY SENSE

- Keep your skateboard properly maintained.
- Wear proper safety equipment, including wrist guards, leather gloves, good elbow and knee pads, long pants, and an approved safety helmet. Since there are no certified skateboard helmets, you should use an approved hockey or bicycle helmet.
- Always skate in a safe place. Skateboarders on television often hitch rides on trucks or jump off ledges. These tricks are not done by amateurs. They are staged events that require good photography and people trained to do stunts. Don't try to imitate them.
- Store your skateboard where other people won't trip over it.
- Never lend your skateboard to anyone who does not know how to ride one.
- Check whether skateboards can be used legally on streets and sidewalks in your municipality.
- Stay away from steep hills. Skateboards can reach very high speeds, causing you to lose control.

Skeet and Trap Shooting

RISK FACTORS
- No North American data are available.

CONTRIBUTING FACTORS
- unauthorized people moving onto the shooting range
- poor shooting skills and techniques
- unsafe gun handling
- recklessness and horseplay

COMMENT

Without question, one of the most attractive aspects of clay target shooting is that nearly anyone can participate. Parents who are reluctant to allow their children to get involved are generally surprised to discover that this is among the safest of shooting sports. It also provides youngsters with an excellent opportunity to develop maturity and self-confidence.

SAFETY SENSE

- The development of good shotgun-handling skills is the major factor in preventing accidents. People with poor skills can become frustrated when missing a target, causing their alertness to decline.
- Always treat a shotgun as if it were loaded. Point the muzzle in a safe direction at all times.
- Keep the shotgun action open except when ready to fire.
- Be completely familiar with how a shotgun operates and what ammunition it uses.
- Carry only one gauge of ammunition so you do not accidentally place a small gauge in the wrong gun.
- Know where your companions are at all times.
- Be sure of your target and of what is beyond the target.
- Never handle any firearm while you are under the influence of alcohol.
- Guns must be cleaned and checked frequently. They should also be checked annually by a gunsmith.
- Only place one shell in the gun at a time, except when shooting double targets.
- If a delay occurs on the range while your gun is loaded, open the action and remove all shells.
- Practice shooting and try firing (shooting without shells) should only

be done on the shooting range or in a designated safe area.

- Place shotguns in an appropriate gun rack or safe area when they are not in use.
- Wear safety glasses and ear protection to protect against hearing damage and flying objects, such as ejecting shells and broken target pieces.
- When ejecting a shell from a gun, point it so that it does not eject into another person's area.
- If a shotgun shell fails to fire, wait five to ten seconds before opening the action. Occasionally a shell may have a slow-burning primer.
- Leave empty shells on the ground until other people are finished shooting.

Spelunking
(Exploring Caves)

RISK FACTORS

- One study showed that some 80 percent of all spelunking accidents involve inexperienced spelunkers.

CONTRIBUTING FACTORS

- inexperience
- falling
- inability to see potential hazards
- falling rocks

COMMENT

Spelunking, the sport of exploring caves, is like mountain climbing underground in the dark. Many of the same obstacles, including high rock walls and narrow ledges, are faced by both spelunkers and mountaineers. Both need endurance, a desire for adventure, and plenty of experience. And both sports can be dangerous unless safety rules are carefully observed.

SAFETY SENSE

- Never go into a cave alone. Use a buddy system.
- Always tell someone outside the cave where you will be and how long you plan to stay there. Be sure to keep to your schedule.
- Mark your route into a cave with arrows pointing back to the entrance. Scratch these arrows in soft mud, chalk them on hard rock, or make them out of small stones.
- Gain spelunking experience in the company of experts or from a course. Practice climbing rocks and using ropes in a safe place before going into a cave.

- Always carry at least three reliable lights. Wear a miner's helmet with a carbide lamp. Carry a flashlight with fresh batteries and candles with plenty of waterproof matches. Be sure to have extra supplies, such as batteries, bulbs, and carbide (a carbon compound that makes the light work).
- You should be in good physical condition so you can withstand the rigors of slithering, crouching, and climbing without injuring yourself.
- Spelunkers need waterproof boots (preferably good hiking boots) and a tight waterproof outer shell that won't

get caught on rocks. Because caves are very warm in the winter, heavy clothing is not necessary.

- Use nylon rope as a lifeline. It stretches if you fall, so it won't jolt you when you hit the end. Nylon rope also resists abrasion. However, all ropes age, so inspect them before each trip. Your life depends on all equipment being in perfect condition.
- Use a sheathed nylon rope for repelling and prussocking (climbing up a rope). The sheath of the rope moves freely, so the rope never twists. Twisting ropes can spin a spelunker out of control.
- Carry high-energy food, such as chocolate, and rest often to avoid fatigue. Fatigue can lead to carelessness and injury.
- Be especially careful of weather conditions. Underground caves can collect groundwater run-off and can become flooded quickly.
- Carbon monoxide poisoning is generally not a problem, but it is good to test the quality of the air as you go along. Light a match, and if it dies instantly, get out of the cave quickly.

Walking

RISK FACTORS
- Fifty-four percent of all pedestrian deaths occur when it is dark.

CONTRIBUTING FACTORS
- reduced visibility for motor vehicle drivers
- poor judgment of distance by motorists and pedestrians
- failure of motorists to see pedestrians
- improperly fitted shoes that cause blisters
- overexertion

COMMENT

Walking is generally safe provided you have properly fitted footwear and you build up your endurance gradually. It is inexpensive, convenient, and healthy. Like all sports, walking helps to reduce stress; it is also relaxing and enjoyable. Walking is good exercise and reduces calories. You can walk the dog, stroll home from work, push a baby stroller, or just walk. Take a walk -- it's fun.

SAFETY SENSE

- Have a physical check-up before beginning a walking program if you are over 40 years of age.
- Always warm up before starting, and walk slowly for the first five to ten minutes. Cool down by going more slowly near the end of the walk and doing some stretching exercises.
- Use a proper walking technique. Keep your head erect, your back straight, your toes pointed ahead, and your arms swinging at your sides. Land on your heel and roll forward off the ball of your foot,

taking long easy strides and breathing deeply and evenly.
- When beginning, walk a flat course, start slowly, and rest when you're tired. Once you are fit, you can increase your distance and your speed.
- Select good walking shoes or jogging shoes. Shop at the end of the day when your feet are larger because you have been on them all day. Most sport stores can help you to select a good shoe.

- Wear retroreflective clothes. When retroreflective materials are not available, wear yellow, white, or light-colored clothing when you walk along a road at night or during dark stormy weather.
- At night, cross roads where lights are bright and visibility is good.
- Walk along the left side of the roadway, facing oncoming traffic, so you can see it and step out of the way.
- Carry a flashlight when walking at night.
- Make use of subways, elevated crosswalks, safety islands, and other safeguards.
- When walking in the winter, snow and ice present additional hazards. Avoid slips and falls by selecting the proper footwear and avoiding icy sidewalks and roadways. Keep a moderate walking pace, with your weight well balanced. If you do fall, relax and roll if you can. Let your whole body absorb the impact.
- In slippery weather, be especially careful when crossing streets since cars cannot make quick stops.
- Don't use ankle or wrist weights when walking. You can easily strain your leg and arm muscles.
- Wear comfortable, flexible, warm, and breathable clothing. Layering is a good way to prevent getting too cold or too warm. In winter, hats, mittens, and waterproof shoes are a must. On especially cold days, wear a facemask or scarf to protect against frostbite. However, don't impair your vision with bulky clothing such as coat hoods.

WATER SPORTS

Millions of people enjoy water activities but, unfortunately, many of them cannot even swim. Data show that 60 percent of drownings in North America occur to people who did not intentionally enter the water.

Water accidents could be significantly reduced if everyone were capable of doing three things:

- swimming well enough to get out of a dangerous situation;
- recognizing and avoiding hazardous practices; and
- having the knowledge and skill to help others in an emergency.

To prevent injury in water-related activities, it is vitally important to understand the causes of water accidents and to know how to prevent them.

Canoeing

RISK FACTORS
- No North American data are available.

CONTRIBUTING FACTORS
- improper stroke techniques and poor conditioning, resulting in injuries, such as shoulder overuse, lower back strain, tendonitis in the wrist, and muscle strains and sprains
- not preparing properly for a trip
- dangerous weather and water conditions
- hypothermia
- sunburn and heat stroke
- dumping the canoe because of poor balance or paddling the canoe in waters too difficult for the canoeist's capability
- poor wilderness survival skills
- poorly maintained or selected equipment

COMMENT

Canoeing is one of North America's most popular forms of outdoor recreation. The most popular form of canoeing is still canoe tripping (touring), involving an excursion of several days or several weeks on inland or coastal waters. Another form is white-water canoeing, which involves paddling in a fast-moving current, through rapids, hydraulics, and ledges. White-water canoeing is considerably more dangerous than canoe tripping. It should be attempted only by experienced canoeists. An increasingly popular form of canoeing is coastal paddling on tidal waters or large bodies of water. Here navigation skills are extremely important, as are skills in paddling in moving water. Canoeists must negotiate tidal waters, waves, swells, varying currents, and other natural hazards.

SAFETY SENSE

- Learn to swim before you try canoeing.
- Always wear an approved life jacket or personal floatation device (PFD) that meets your body size requirements.
- Take a canoeing course from a professional.

- Maintain all equipment properly and select the appropriate equipment for the type of canoeing you will do.
- Wear a helmet when paddling in moving water.
- Ensure that you plan carefully for a long trip before starting out. Establish your route, locate camping areas, determine where to put in and take out your canoe, set your approximate time of arrival, and have a back-up plan in case of emergency.
- Inform someone, perhaps the police or a friend, of your estimated time of arrival.
- Don't get into situations beyond your capability.
- Never swim away from a capsized canoe. It will float and eventually reach shore.
- Carry a spare paddle and a bucket or can for bailing excess water.
- Watch the weather for approaching thunderstorms.
- Do not paddle through thunderstorms. Instead, seek shelter on shore.
- In sudden wind squalls or rough water, sit in the bottom of the canoe, keeping your center of gravity as low as possible.
- Never try to canoe over a dam.
- Do not change places in a canoe.
- Carry a small, collapsible anchor with you. If you lose your paddle and begin drifting, you may end up in serious trouble.
- Know the water along the route that you will take. Check for obstacles, rapids, and other potential hazards.
- Protect your eyes and body from the sun. Wear sunglasses, long sleeves, and long trousers to prevent sunburn and sunstroke.

Diving

RISK FACTORS
- Over 99.9 percent of diving-related injuries occur outside a supervised public facility.
- It is estimated that over 13,000 people annually in North America are medically treated for diving and diving board injuries.

CONTRIBUTING FACTORS
- striking the bottom, a slope, or an object in the water
- diving into the shallow end of pools
- ignoring depth markings
- attempting dives beyond the diver's ability
- stricking the diving board

COMMENT

Water sports, particularly diving, are chief causes of cervical spine injuries resulting in quadriplegia. The typical victim is a male in his teens or early twenties and a first-time visitor to the area in which the accident occurred.

SAFETY SENSE

- Beginners should enroll in a certified diving course where they learn to respect the water.
- Never dive into water that is less than 3 m (10 ft.) deep. When diving, the average person plunges into the water at a rate of 1.2 m (4 ft.) per second. At that speed, you can seriously injure yourself if you hit something solid.
- Never dive into a backyard pool, or above-ground pool, even if there is a diving board because they are usually too shallow.
- Never dive in unfamiliar water.
- Even if you are familiar with the water, you should still walk in the first time to determine whether there are any hidden objects and to measure the depth of the water. As well, watch out for strong currents and drop-offs.
- Only one person should be on a diving board at a time.
- Do not dive from the side of the board.
- Do not bounce the diving board excessively or fool around on it.
- Do not hang or swing by your arms from a high board.
- Make sure the diver in front of you is out of your way before diving. Once you are in the water, keep away from the board.

Fishing

RISK FACTORS

- Over 90 percent of all anglers who die in water-related accidents are not wearing life jackets or personal floatation devices (PFDs).
- Alcohol is involved in 33 percent of all fishing fatalities.

CONTRIBUTING FACTORS

- hooking yourself or others with a lure
- bites from fish
- drowning
- drinking alcohol
- falling from riverbanks, cliffs, etc.
- wading in unknown waters
- hypothermia
- failing to wear a life jacket or PFD

COMMENT

Fishing is one of the most popular outdoor sports. It requires only simple equipment, and the relative isolation of lakes and streams in North America make it a relaxing sport for millions of people. Most fishing hazards are related to poor swimming skills, the improper use of fishing equipment, and failing to wear a life jacket or PFD at all times.

SAFETY SENSE

- Fishing and drinking alcohol don't mix.
- Check the weather forecast before you set out. Protect yourself from hypothermia. See Special Topics, page 218 for safety sense tips on hypothermia.
- Always wear a life jacket or PFD when fishing in a lake or deep river.
- Learn to swim -- it's never too late.
- Know the body of water in which you plan to fish. Talk to someone familiar with the area, such as local anglers or people in fishing shops.
- Keep off undercut riverbanks. Walk well back from weeds and tall grasses along the water's edge. They can give a false impression of where the edge actually is.
- When wading, always watch out for spots where your feet might become trapped. If you fall down with your feet trapped, the current can push you under and hold you there.
- Be very cautious on rocks and other slippery surfaces. Wear felt-soled waders for traction on wet rocks. Use a staff or long-handled net to help you keep your balance.
- Keep your feet apart in fast water and lean into the current, taking small steps.
- Always face slightly upstream while crossing the current.

- Wear a belt around your waist if you are wearing hip-waders. This will help prevent water from entering the boots.
- If you fall into the water while wearing waders, do not panic and do not attempt to swim. Rather, tuck up your knees immediately to reduce the amount of water entering the waders and to trap air, which will make you more buoyant. Roll onto your back, throw back your head, and paddle backward with your arms toward shore.
- Release the slack on your line when removing weeds or changing lures.

A bowed rod can snap a hook into your body.
- Cast carefully and always pay attention to where other people are standing. Do not cast side-arm when others are standing near you.
- If a hook catches in your flesh, push the barb through, then cut it off. For this purpose, always carry a pair of wire-cutting pliers in your tackle box. Attend to the wound immediately.
- Handle fish carefully. Sharp teeth or fins can cause considerable pain.
- Refer to other units in this section for safe boating practices.

Kayaking

RISK FACTORS
- No North American data are available. However, based on limited North American information, it is estimated that 40 people per year die in kayaking accidents. Most of these people drown.

CONTRIBUTING FACTORS
- exceeding your level of ability
- submerged paddler being pinned between rock and the overturned, water-filled boat
- boat getting pinned on rocks, logs, or trees
- extremely high run-off
- striking your head on submerged rocks
- drowning
- hypothermia
- poorly maintained equipment

COMMENT

The sport of kayaking has grown tremendously in the past 20 years. It offers challenge, excitement, and good exercise to people who have the knowledge and physical skills required.

Kayakers can navigate rivers with swift currents and rapids that would capsize most boats. To people who are not sufficiently skilled, kayaking can be dangerous or even fatal. Safe kayaking demands that people keep to water conditions that are appropriate for their skills.

SAFETY SENSE

- Take a kayaking course from a professional.
- Kayak in groups of two or more; never go alone.
- Carry a throw rope or a rescue bag.
- Always wear a helmet and a life jacket or personal floatation device (PFD).
- Ensure that your floatation bags are inflated.
- Check water levels and the difficulty of your route before setting out.
- Scout all unfamiliar rapids for hazards.
- Beware of heavy run-off and spring floods.
- Dress adequately for the conditions and for an unexpected swim.
- Resist the impulse to push your limits or the limits of your less experienced companions.
- All kayakers must learn self-rescue techniques, including how to maneuvre upstream of a drifting boat.

- Refer to page 218 for safety sense tips on hypothermia. All kayakers should wear thermal clothing if the water temperature is below 8° C (46° F).
- It is important to be alert. Never use alcoholic beverages or medication before or during your trip.
- Select routes that are patrolled by safety spotters and power boats. You never know when an emergency will occur.

- If you kayak in open water, such as the ocean, you need special knowledge and instruction. Ocean kayakers face conditions that are changeable and, to some extent, unpredictable. Sea winds, tidal currents, and ocean swells can cause accidents. You must also have the navigational skills to use charts, a compass, and a trained eye to keep yourself out of trouble.

RISK FACTORS

- It is estimated that more than 90 percent of people in North America who drown are occupants of small boats.
- Light, highly maneuverable boats account for more deaths than other types of boats.
- Motorized boats contribute to 75 percent of the fatalities.
- Approximately 42 percent of victims in boating accidents had been drinking alcohol.

CONTRIBUTING FACTORS

- travelling too fast for water or weather conditions
- drinking alcohol
- failing to follow safe boating rules and regulations
- overloading the boat
- carelessness
- dangerous weather conditions
- inexperience
- improper installation and maintenance of equipment
- failing to wear life jackets or personal floatation devices (PFDs)

COMMENT

The popularity of recreational boating in North America has continued to grow for many years. About one in seven households owns some type of recreational boat. One of four North Americans goes boating each year, making it one of the most popular family recreational activities. Whether they use a boat for fishing, to get supplies to the family cottage, or just as a means to escape from the world for a while, boaters should learn to use their crafts safely.

With so many boaters on the waterways today, enforcement officials and safety professionals are increasing their efforts to educate boaters about safe boating rules and regulations. Since operator error is the most significant factor contributing to boating accidents, the need for education is great.

- Boats and alcoholic drinks don't mix. Like driving a vehicle or flying an airplane, boating under the influence of alcohol is against the law.
- Make sure that every person on board the boat wears life jackets or PFDs at all times.
- Move around in the boat carefully. Better yet, remain seated and enjoy the ride.
- Keep an eye out for storms. Check weather conditions before leaving, and carry a radio with you to receive regular weather reports.
- Learn to swim.
- Recklessness on board a boat is just plain stupid. Never allow anyone to ride in the bow. Keep all passengers in their seats.
- Do not overpower your boat by exceeding its horsepower rating. Overpowered boats are very unstable and can capsize when turning.
- Be prepared to handle big waves and sudden squalls.
- As a boat operator, you're responsible for your craft while it's on the water. Power-driven boats should always give the right of way to sailboats, canoes, rowboats, and other boats without motors.
- It pays to be a weight-watcher. Too much weight -- caused by too many people, too much gear, or too large a motor -- can capsize or sink even the most seaworthy craft.
- In most jurisdictions throughout North America, the minimum safety equipment required by regulation for pleasure boats (8 to 12 m/26 to 40 ft.) is the following:
  - one approved small-vessel life jacket or PFD for each person on board;
  - one approved life buoy, 762 or 610 mm (30 or 24 in.) in diameter;
  - one buoyant heaving line at least

15 m (49 ft.) long;
  - twelve approved pyrotechnic distress signals, of which not more than six may be daylight smoke signals;
  - one anchor with at least 15 m (49 ft.) of cable, rope, or chain;
  - one Class BII fire extinguisher;
  - one bailer (bucket or can) and one manual bilge pump; and
  - navigation lights and a sound signalling system.
- Boats not longer than 5.5 m (18 ft.) must carry a life jacket or PFD for each person, two oars or paddles, one hand-held bailer or manual pump, a class BI fire extinguisher (if the boat has an inboard motor or built-in fuel tanks), navigation lights, and a sound signalling system.
- Never refuel any boat while passengers are on board. Extinguish all smoking material and open flames before refuelling. Take portable tanks to shore. Do not operate electrical switches while refuelling, and clean up all spillage afterward.
- Never leave your mooring until you have checked your boat thoroughly.
- Always be courteous, careful, and competent. Be considerate about your boat wash. Slow down to 6 km/h (4 mph) in harbors.
- Keep away from large vessels; they are not as maneuvrable as small boats.
- Water bikes, or jet skis, are subject to the same regulations as motorboats in most jurisdictions.
- Keep away from swimming areas.
- Always approach the dock or mooring against the wind or current, whichever is stronger. This will give you more control over your boat.
- Contact your local coast guard office for additional information on safe boating.

Rowing

RISK FACTORS
- No North American data are available.

CONTRIBUTING FACTORS
- drowning
- muscle strain due to overexertion
- being hit by oars
- heat-related injuries, including heatstroke
- hypothermia
- poorly maintained equipment

COMMENT

Rowing was once an important means of transportation. Today, it is a popular sport and an excellent form of exercise. You can row a simple rowboat or join a rowing club that offers single sculling and team racing. Whichever type of rowing you do, follow these basic safety sense suggestions.

SAFETY SENSE

- Know how to swim and use a life jacket or personal floatation device (PFD).
- Monitor the weather forecast and, if bad weather approaches, head for shore immediately.
- Let someone know your estimated return time and your approximate route.
- Check the boat and equipment, including oar locks, oars, and the anchor, to make sure they are in good condition.
- Use lights on your boat before sunrise and after dark.
- Have a complete safety kit in each boat. The kit should contain a bailer, an anchor, an extra line, oars, a first-aid kit, a flare kit, and any other equipment that may be useful during your excursion.
- On shells, install bow balls to prevent the sharp nose from injuring someone.
- Equip all shells with quick-release shoes, either velcro closing or heel tie-down styles.
- Equip shells with horns and whistles.
- Know the following distress signals:
  - waving your arms;
  - waving a shirt overhead;
  - blowing a whistle or horn; and
  - raising one oar vertically to the boat.

- Do not swim away from a swamped or capsized boat. Use an oar or the boat to keep you afloat.
- Use the buddy system **at all times** when not accompanied by a launch. Scullers should not go out alone.
- Stay within reach of the shore if you are alone in a shell.
- Refer to page 218 for safety sense tips on hypothermia.
- When rowing in hot, humid weather, drink enough fluids to replace the amount your body loses. Do not take salt tablets. Drink plenty of water before, during, and after rowing.
- Know the signs of heat exhaustion (extreme weakness, headache, nausea, vomiting, muscle cramps, and pale, clammy skin).
- Stop and check your position often when rowing blind (with your back to the direction of travel). A power boat should accompany boaters in a shell.
- Be especially careful when transporting a shell out of the water. The oars or the bow could hit someone and cause an injury.

RISK FACTORS
- The most common causes of fatalities are drowning or dying from hypothermia after capsizing or being thrown overboard.

CONTRIBUTING FACTORS
- failing to monitor weather changes and to adjust the rigging appropriately
- running into power lines
- high winds
- inexperience
- failing to maintain backup power equipment and getting stranded
- hypothermia
- boat capsizing
- failing to wear a life jacket or personal floatation device (PFD)
- being hit by the boom
- getting fingers caught in winches or blocks
- poorly maintained equipment

COMMENT

Fewer lives are lost in sailboat accidents than accidents involving other types of small craft. One factor is that most people learn to sail in organized schools where safety is stressed. Another factor could be that sailing demands close attention and constant physical activity -- sailors are more likely to be attentive. People who sail are more prepared to fall into the water than other people operating small craft.

SAFETY SENSE

- Every sailboat crew should establish emergency procedures and practice them until everyone knows exactly what to do.
- When someone falls overboard, the captain must bring the boat motionless in the water, while designated crew members recover the person.
- If someone falls overboard at night, it is important for the boat to be as visible as possible to the person overboard. Shine floodlighting on the sails using an emergency battery-powered lantern or by shooting up a parachute illuminating flare.
- If the crew cannot right a capsized boat, they should float with it rather than swim away.
- Sails that are fouled so they cannot be released quickly in sudden squalls or unexpected rough wea-

ther are a common cause of capsizing.

- Survival suits should be carried on sailboats that go out to sea or far out on large lakes. Cold water can kill unprotected people. Stow the suits where they can be recovered easily, even on a foundering boat. Refer to page 218 for safety sense tips on hypothermia.
- Never consume alcohol when under sail or before sailing time.
- When underway, sailboat crews should continuously monitor the marine distress frequency on the radio.
- Listen to weather forecasts before and during your sailing trip.

- Wear a safety harness on a large boat in medium and high winds.
- Instruct passengers on what to do when a boat is tacking and when the boom swings.
- Invest in up-to-date nautical charts. These can save your boat from damage and may even save your life.
- Before setting sail, make a complete check of all safety equipment and emergency gear noting their condition in the log. Do not set out until any serious deficiencies are corrected.
- Know the different types of lines used on your boat and how to tie and maintain them correctly.

Skin Diving and Scuba Diving

RISK FACTORS
- It is estimated that 80 people die annually in North America as a result of skin diving and scuba diving.

CONTRIBUTING FACTORS
- poorly maintained equipment
- losing consciousness following an injury
- drowning
- running out of tank air
- hyperventilating
- incorrect ascent and descent
- inexperience
- exceeding your personal abilities

COMMENT

Skin diving and scuba diving give you the feeling of complete freedom and weight-lessness under water. You have the sensation of flying as you glide by spectacular scenery. Whether you want to go skin diving (using a snorkel) or scuba diving (using a self-contained underwater breathing apparatus), the dangers of the sport can be overcome by taking a certified instructional course.

SAFETY SENSE

- Enroll in a diving course offered by a certifying organization and taught by a certified underwater instructor.
- Do not use alcohol or medication before diving.
- Have a regular medical examination.
- Use correct, complete, and well-maintained diving equipment. Never lend your equipment to an uncertified diver.
- If you dive in open water, use personal floatation (cartridge-type) equipment, plus a submersible pressure gauge or a reserve warning mechanism and wet suits.
- Know the limitations of your abilities and your equipment. Allow a margin of safety so you are prepared for emergencies. Set moderate limits for depth and time in the water.
- Use a buddy system when diving.
- Learn about your diving location in advance. Avoid dangerous places and poor conditions, such as underwater caves, reefs, and undertows.

- Control your buoyancy to make diving as easy as possible. Be prepared to ditch your weights and make an emergency ascent. Remember, however, that fast ascents may cause the "bends."
- In an emergency, don't panic. Stop and think. Get control and then take action.
- Learn hand signals and stay in contact with your partner.
- Use a boat or float as a surface support station whenever possible.
- Use the international scuba marker to show boats and others on the surface of the water that a diver is below.
- Breathe continuously throughout the dive; avoid over-breathing or hyperventilating.
- Be sure to equalize pressure early and often, both during ascent and descent, to prevent the "bends."
- Know decompression procedures, tables on how quickly you can come up from a deep dive, and emergency procedures.
- If you are cold, tired, or not feeling well, get out of the water immediately.

- If using underwater equipment, such as a spear gun, make sure it is working properly and use it safely.
- Make sure you know how to "buddy breath" (share an air tank with another diver) in an emergency.
- High-pressure cylinders or tanks are potentially the most dangerous equipment you use. Inspect them often. Hydrostatic inspections should be done at least once very five years. Store your tanks safely.
- All divers must pass a basic swimming course and have a medical examination.
- Never dive if you have a head cold and never wear earplugs. Pressure will build up inside your ears, causing severe injury.
- Snorkelling equipment should include a well-fitting face mask with a tempered glass face plate. Fins should have strong straps that won't break. Snorkel tubes should be shaped so that they are easy to breathe through.
- Do not use snorkel tubes with ball valves. These valves sometimes get stuck, cutting off the air supply.

Surfing

RISK FACTORS

• It is estimated that approximately 2,000 people in North America are treated annually for injuries received while surfing.

CONTRIBUTING FACTORS

• carelessness
• inexperience
• being hit by a loose board
• hitting bottom in shallow water
• congested surfing area

COMMENT

Relatively few fatalities result from surfing accidents. The greatest speed that a surfer travels is 40 to 50 km/h (25 to 30 mph). Experienced surfers can generally minimize any disaster by maneuvering their boards so that they will not collide with another surfer's plunging or flying board.

SAFETY SENSE

• Do not use a surfboard unless you can swim well.
• Surf in an area that is not congested by other surfers or swimmers. The area should also be free of rock jetties, wooden bulkheads, and buoys.
• Wear protective equipment. A growing number of surfers regularly use safety equipment, including a lightweight helmet, an inflated or foam water-skiing belt and a surf leash, which saves the surfer a long swim to recover the board.
• If you are going to fall off your surfboard dive back into the wave, not away from the wave. The wave will provide more water in which to land. The water in front of the wave may be very shallow.

RISK FACTORS

- It is estimated that every year approximately 2,000 people in North America drown while swimming. About 25 percent of these deaths occur in home swimming pools.

CONTRIBUTING FACTORS

- poor supervision
- failing to avoid dangerous areas
- poor swimming skills
- failing to wear life jackets or personal floatation devices (PFDs) for nonswimmers
- being struck in the water by boats or other objects
- fatigue and overexertion

COMMENT

Swimming is one of the most healthy sports. Nearly every muscle of the body is used in swimming, and regular swimming helps develop coordination and strength. Millions of people swim regularly in rivers, lakes, oceans, and pools. If you don't know how to swim, take a certified course now. You never know when it will save your life.

SAFETY SENSE

- Never swim alone; use the buddy system.
- Adjust your body to the temperature of the water slowly by taking a shower or splashing your body with water.
- Do not swim right after eating a heavy meal or you may get cramps.
- Avoid swimming if you have infectious viruses, skin allergies, or any communicable illness.
- Never push or throw anyone into the water.
- Swim only in areas that are well supervised.

- Never let nonswimmers near or in the water without an approved life jacket or PFD.
- Do not swim past safety buoy markers.
- Before swimming, always determine the depth of the water and check for potential hazards such as drop-offs.
- Swimming in rivers poses special risks due to currents and debris on the bottom.
- Overexertion is a major factor contributing to injuries. Take frequent rest breaks.

- Never swim during a thunderstorm or for 15 minutes before or afterward because of possibility of being struck by lightning.
- In the ocean, swim with the waves and avoid heavy surf. Watch out for undertow and stay on the surface of the water.
- Stay out of areas used by boaters and surfers.
- Many serious injuries occur when people run on pool decks, which are slippery when wet.
- Never swim after drinking alcoholic beverages or taking medication.
- Check all swimming areas carefully before entering the water.

Synchronized Swimming

RISK FACTORS
- No North American data are available.

CONTRIBUTING FACTORS
- hyperventilation
- overexertion
- sprains and strains to knees and shoulders
- overtraining
- falling on the pool deck
- failing to warm up

COMMENT

Most injuries in synchronized swimming can be prevented by advance planning, including a gradual strength-training program that should become an integral part of the swimmer's routine.

SAFETY SENSE

- Learn the safety procedures to use in and around the pool.
- Learn the proper use and care of equipment.
- Warm up before starting a routine.
- Decrease or stop training after an injury and return gradually to training.
- Have a yearly medical checkup.
- Inform the coach of any changes in general health, of infectious viruses, and of skin allergies.
- Plan a training schedule that is appropriate for your age and level of development.
- Develop general fitness before working on specific synchronized swimming skills.
- The program should be progressive, based on the coach's technical knowledge to prevent unnecessary injuries.

Tubing

RISK FACTORS
• No North American data are available.

CONTRIBUTING FACTORS
• drowning
• hitting obstacles on the river
• failing to wear protective equipment
• sunstroke
• hypothermia
• failing to use a pickup partner
• drinking alcohol
• poorly maintained equipment

COMMENT

Tubing leisurely down a slow, winding river or rushing down a white-water river is exhilarating. Like all water sports, however, tubing involves hazards, most of which are controllable by the tuber. Learn the techniques of tubing and read about the sport before attempting your first ride.

SAFETY SENSE

• To protect your body, wear jeans, canvas shoes, a helmet, sport safety sunglasses, a long-sleeved shirt, and sunburn lotion.
• Carry a compact first-aid kit and high-energy food with you -- you may end up staying overnight on shore due to an injury or slow-moving water.
• Carry plenty of drinking water on hot, humid days.
• Never go tubing in water that is colder than 8° C (46° F) without a wet suit. Refer to page 218 for safety sense tips on hypothermia.
• Never tube alone. Many things could go wrong.
• Always have a pick up partner at the end of your tubing run. Your pick up partner will return you to your point of origin. If you do not reach your destination at the appointed time, your pick up partner will search for you and will follow emergency procedures to ensure that you are found.
• Become an accomplished swimmer before taking up tubing.
• Always wear a life jacket or a personal floatation device (PFD).
• Never drink alcoholic beverages before or during a trip. You will need all your mental and physical skills to handle the river.
• Do a complete check of all equipment before your trip, and take repair materials and equipment with you.

Water Polo

RISK FACTORS
- No North American data are available.

CONTRIBUTING FACTORS
- getting hit in the face by the ball or by an opponent's hands or feet
- getting angry and losing self-control
- jamming your fingers or thumbs
- matching experienced players against less skillful opponents
- poor physical conditioning
- improper playing and swimming techniques
- overexertion
- failing to warm up

COMMENT

Water polo was invented in England in the 1870s. In 1900, it was introduced into the Olympic games. Water polo combines swimming and throwing, both of which can cause injuries, especially to knees and shoulders.

SAFETY SENSE

- All players should keep their fingernails trimmed and remove rings and jewelry that may injure fellow players.
- Observe the rules of the game. Holding or kicking can lead to rough play and fights, which can lead to injury.
- Goalkeepers should wear lightweight face masks.
- A physical conditioning program for knees, thighs, lower back, shoulders, pelvis, and hips is very important in preventing injury.

- Warm-up programs are essential for water polo players.
- All players should have medical examinations by a physician who specializes in sports medicine.
- Swimming strains all your muscles. Know when to rest and do not overtrain.
- Lacerations to the face and forehead are common in water polo. Make every effort to protect your face from injury. Wearing ear and head protection will prevent injuries to the head.

RISK FACTORS

- It is estimated that approximately 24,000 people are treated annually in North America for water-skiing injuries. An average of 27 people die each year as a result of these injuries.

CONTRIBUTING FACTORS

- inexperience
- recklessness
- fatigue
- untrained tow operator
- poor swimming skills
- failing to wear a life jacket or personal floatation device (PFD)
- failing to have an observer in the tow boat
- falling
- striking objects in the water or on land
- skiing at night
- poorly maintained equipment

COMMENT

When you combine a speeding boat, water, and water skis, you have the potential for mishap. However, deaths and serious injuries from water-skiing have been few, largely due to the use of commonsense safety practices.

SAFETY SENSE

- It is unsafe for two people to ski together using ropes of different lengths. The longer rope could entangle the other skier after a fall.
- Always wear a life jacket or PFD.
- Learn to swim well before you try water-skiing.
- Beginners should take lessons to prevent unnecessary injuries.
- All skiers must learn the basic hand signals to communicate with the boat observer and operator. Holding up a ski or clasping your hands over your head signals that all is well and ensures that other boaters see you in the water.
- Skiers should keep away from solid objects, such as docks, boats, and tree stumps.
- Skiers should watch the boat at all times. There should be an observer in the boat.
- Never put any part of your body through the bridle of the tow rope or wrap the line around yourself.

- Wearing protective equipment, such as gloves, a helmet, and a PFD, will help prevent skiing injuries.
- Never ski at night.
- Never ski so long that you become exhausted.
- Learn to get to shore safely. When landing, slowly ski in parallel to the shore. Landing accidents cause more than half of all water-skiing injuries.
- If you have a choice, fall backward. If you fall forward, ankle and knee injuries can result from the extra leverage produced by the tips of the skis digging into the water.
- Many injuries occur when the boat starts out because the driver accelerates before the skier is ready.
- Propellers on any type of boat should be treated with proper respect. Never get on an outboard or stern-driven boat from the back of the boat even when the power is off. A slip could cause your foot or leg to get cut on a propeller blade.

- The safety of the skier is the driver's primary responsibility. When you are the driver, avoid sharp turns and other maneuvres that might cause the skier to fall. Drive with the skier's ability in mind. Bring the boat about as promptly as possible when a skier falls.
- The driver can reduce the chance of landing accidents by slowing down the boat before the skier releases the handle.
- Avoid areas where there are swimmers, fishermen, boats, or other obstructions.
- Check skiing equipment thoroughly. Repair loose runners or torn bindings, and eliminate sharp or protruding objects on the skis.
- If you are in the boat, handle tow lines carefully; they can cause torn muscles, rope burns, and even the loss of fingers and toes.
- Replace tow lines that are frayed and in danger of breaking.

RISK FACTORS

- It is estimated that five to ten injuries occur for every 100,000 trips down a water slide.
- Approximately 5,000 people in North America are treated annually for injuries received while playing on home water slides.

CONTRIBUTING FACTORS

- collisions between sliders
- inadequate spacing between sliders
- hitting the bottom of the pool
- colliding with flume walls at turns
- poorly maintained equipment

COMMENT

Water slides take riders down a straight or curved course into a pool of water. There must be a continuous flow of water over the surface of the slide to reduce friction. Slides are fun for adults as well as children, especially on hot days. When you are supervising children who are sliding, contribute to their fun by establishing some safety sense rules that will reduce the likelihood of injury.

SAFETY SENSE

- Ensure that there is adequate space between you and the slider ahead. It is almost impossible to stop once you've started down the slide.
- Never slide in tandem (two or more people holding on to each other).
- At the exit end, clear the slide area immediately to prevent collisions with sliders coming down after you.
- Go slow on your first slide, and look for rough spots, fast corners, protruding bolts, and weldings. All these things can cause abrasions and other injuries.

- Always go feet first into the pool to prevent head injuries.
- Absolutely no horseplay should be allowed by slide supervisors. Users not abiding by the safety rules should be banned from the water slide.
- When putting down a ground slide (a plastic strip covered with water), ensure that it is placed in a safe location and that the hold-down pegs are not protruding above ground. Teach children the correct way to use the ground slide.

White-Water Rafting

RISK FACTORS
- No North American data are available. However, one review showed that one treatable injury occurs for every 2,000 hours of rafting.

CONTRIBUTING FACTORS
- drowning
- inexperience
- hitting obstructions on the river
- being thrown from the raft
- hand blisters and minor strains
- hypothermia
- poorly maintained equipment

COMMENT

White-water rafting is done on rivers where the water is rushing among obstacles, such as trees and rocks. The resulting turbulence can create complicated water movements. The raft can be dashed about in sudden changes of speed and direction.

White-water rafting has exploded in popularity as a recreational activity in North America. The sport is really for adults; the normal minimum age for white-water rafting is 16 years old. Be prepared to sign a liability waiver before taking a trip. You may also be required to state your medical fitness.

SAFETY SENSE

- Choose a reliable white-water rafting operator whose equipment is in good shape.
- Pad the frame of the raft and eliminate sharp projections that could cause injury.
- Use strong oars or paddles that are big enough to control the raft. Carry several spares.
- Never go in a raft without life jackets or personal floatation devices (PFDs). Carry at least one extra life jacket per raft.
- Do not overload the raft.
- Carry bow and stern lines and a rescue line. Check to ensure that ropes are arranged so that they won't entangle passengers if the raft overturns.
- Carry materials to repair the raft, including an air pump.
- Know your rafting ability and do not attempt rivers beyond your skill.
- The raft should be controlled by someone who knows the river well. Remember that very small changes in water level can change the currents and hazards.

- Dress appropriately for the weather and water temperature. Wear tennis shoes that will protect your feet if you are thrown into the river or if you are forced to walk for help.
- Learn how to escape from an overturned raft. If you are being swept through rapids, lean back on your life jacket and keep your legs up.
- Carry first-aid supplies. If the trip will carry you into remote areas, carry survival equipment.
- File your rafting plans with the appropriate authorities or with someone who will contact those authorities after a specified time. Determine where assistance is available along the river in case of an emergency.
- Wear a wet suit if the water temperature is below 8° C (46° F). Refer to page 218 for safety sense tips on hypothermia.
- Wear a helmet at all times.

Windsurfing (Board Sailing)

RISK FACTORS
- No North American data are available. However, reports from sailors indicate that knee, foot, and ankle injuries are common and mostly related to the foot straps which transfer stresses from the board to the leg areas.

CONTRIBUTING FACTORS
- exhaustion
- hypothermia
- failing to wear life jackets or personal floatation devices (PFDs)
- failing to use a safety leash
- inexperience
- poor physical conditioning
- failure to warm up
- poorly maintained equipment

COMMENT

The best way to choose a windsurfing board is to follow advice from a professional. A good windsurfing school can provide information on and samples of several types of boards for you to choose from.

Taking lessons also enables you to learn windsurfing more safely and more quickly than if you start on your own. The sport demands mastery of a basic technique and, unless you learn it well, your progress will be difficult. With a few hours of lessons, you can learn to navigate in an average wind without developing bad habits. Lessons will also enable you to find out whether you like windsurfing before spending thousands of dollars on the sport.

SAFETY SENSE

- Windsurfing lessons are essential for beginner windsurfers.
- You must know how to rescue yourself by furling the sail, placing your mast and sail on top of the board, lying on your stomach, and paddling your board to safety.
- Go windsurfing in an area supervised by a rescue boat.
- If the water is cold, wear a wetsuit, waterproof boots or shoes, a hat, and gloves. You will need the insulation to prevent hypothermia if you fall in the water. Refer to page 218 for safety sense tips on hypothermia.
- Be aware of offshore breezes, those that come from the land. You may not be able to return to shore.
- Never go windsurfing alone.
- Know the hazards and the depths of the water where you will be sailing. Hazards, such as currents, rocks,

and tides, can pose special problems.
- Take frequent rest breaks. Overexertion invites injuries and accidents.
- Wear polarized lenses to help reduce glare and eye burn. Glass
must be impact-resistant and feature
a padded or rubber bridge.

- To prevent back injury, make sure
your harness fits snugly and doesn't
move around. Remember, the lower
you place the support hook, the
better the support for your lower
back.
- Never sail after drinking alcohol or
taking medication.

FIELD SPORTS

Although interest in sports and recreation has had its most visible expression in the unprecedented growth of individual sports and fitness programs, organized team sports are also spreading widely. In the past, team sports were dominated by serious male athletes. Now participants are frequently men, women, and youth with no previous experience in the sport. Although the skill level of the experienced athlete and the novice may be quite different, they share similar needs for fitness training and injury prevention.

Field sports provide a special challenge to individual players, who frequently cannot set the limits of their participation according to their own fitness or fatigue level, because team pressure to continue play often takes precedence. In addition, many amateur athletes are haphazard in their fitness training for field sports. Unfortunately, many recreational leagues have a beer keg at the sidelines, which may increase the risks of injury. Poor fitness levels, rusty techniques, and a casual approach to sports competition all set the stage for serious injury. But, with some guidelines for fitness and safety, field sports can usually be injury-free.

Baseball

RISK FACTORS
- It is estimated that over 344,000 people are medically treated in North America for injuries received while participating in organized and unorganized baseball.
- Nearly 20 percent of injuries to little league players are to the face, eyes, and mouth.

CONTRIBUTING FACTORS
- being struck by the ball
- colliding with other players
- colliding with field obstacles (bases, fences, and so on)
- failing to wear protective equipment
- poor physical conditioning
- failing to warm up

COMMENT

Although few fatalities occur to players or spectators in the sport of baseball, many serious and minor injuries do occur. The hazards involved are running, body contact, balls thrown or hit hard, bats swung or thrown, and obstacles in the field.

SAFETY SENSE

- The use of a fully protective batter's helmet by all players, both in organized and unorganized baseball games, would help to eliminate most ear and skull injuries. Helmets should provide protection to the top, sides and back of the head, and must fit snugly.
- When playing as a catcher, you must wear a helmet including a face mask, preferably attached to the helmet itself to protect your whole head.
- Steel spike baseball shoes should not be used in little league baseball.
- Female little league players should wear a protective girdle and male players should wear a personal protector (cup) to protect the groin.
- Locate the on-deck circle and the dugout, if they are used, behind a screened area in order to prevent injuries from foul balls or thrown bats. This is especially important for little league play.
- In little league games, you must use breakaway bases.
- Avoid wearing sunglasses, which can shatter if you are hit with a ball. Learn how to shield your eyes from the sun with your glove.
- Make sure you do a 20-minute warm-up of legs and arms to prevent muscle strains.
- The outfield fence should be made of a flexible material to absorb impact when it is hit by a player.

- Warning tracks should be in place around the outfield to provide a clue for the players as to when they are approaching the fence.
- In sandlot play, inspect the field area for potholes, broken glass, and other obstacles and debris.
- It is inadvisable to slide into bases, particularly in sandlot baseball.
- If you do slide, make sure you know safe, correct sliding techniques. **Never slide head first**. In some cases, sliding can help you avoid being hit by a ball because you are low and partly out of the way. It can also prevent a collision with the base person.
- Keep your eyes on the ball at all times to avoid being hit. This is particularly important when you are at bat.
- When playing in the infield, always tag the runner with the back of the glove to save your fingers from being jammed. Improper tagging can also result in sprained and broken wrists.
- Coordinate your signals with other fielders to prevent collisions when making plays in the field.
- To reduce baseball injuries to young players, enroll them in an organized baseball program where coaches are trained and certified to teach proper techniques and skills.

Equestrian Jumping

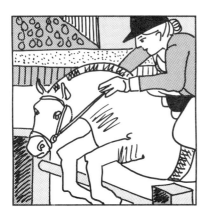

RISK FACTORS

- Falls from horses account for approximately 65 percent of the reported riding accidents.
- One study indicates that 33 percent of horse-related deaths result from head injuries.

CONTRIBUTING FACTORS

- falls
- failing to wear protective head gear
- riding an inexperienced horse
- inexperienced rider
- poorly maintained equipment

COMMENT

Equestrian jumping refers to the sport of jumping a horse over barriers such as fences. There are plenty of risks in the sport, especially when you consider that a 675 kg (1,500 lb.) horse may come trampling down on you. The most important skill to learn to prevent serious injury in this sport is how to fall properly.

SAFETY SENSE

- Wear clothing that is appropriate for the sport -- snug-fitting clothing, gloves to protect your hands, and leather boots with smooth soles and heels.
- You must wear protective head gear while riding, according to equestrian rules and regulations. Approved protection includes a chin strap and a shock-resistant visor. It is extremely important that the chin strap is tightened correctly.
- The saddle should fit the horse properly and there should be good pads under the saddle.
- Do not use stirrups that are too large or too small; your feet may either become stuck or slip through the stirrups.
- Make sure the bridle and bit fit the horse properly.
- Keep yourself and the horse calm and make sure you are relaxed at all times when jumping.
- If you are a beginner, make sure you have coaching and learn the techniques on an experienced horse.
- You will avoid many injuries if you know how to fall properly. As soon as you begin to fall, turn palms toward each other and bend elbows to take the landing shock on the side of your arm and shoulder; tuck your chin into your chest and roll over on either shoulder.
- Make sure that the horse's hooves are trimmed and that its shoes fit properly.

Field Hockey

RISK FACTORS
- It is estimated that over 6,000 people are medically treated in North America each year for injuries received while playing field hockey.
- In one study, it was reported that the ball and stick account for 47 percent of all injuries.
- An international study showed that 50 percent of players own a mouth protector, but less than 25 percent actually wear it during practice or play.

CONTRIBUTING FACTORS
- banging heads together
- colliding with other players
- being hit by the ball or stick
- falls
- poor physical conditioning
- overexertion and fatigue
- poorly maintained equipment

COMMENT

Field hockey is a sport played by both men and women in schools, sports clubs, and Olympic competition. Although it is not well-known in North America, field hockey is played in nearly 100 countries.

The game is played on a soccer-sized pitch (field). Like soccer, it demands a high level of physical conditioning. Running speed, stamina, and stick-handling skills are all important. Consideration for other players and some safety sense are necessary to minimize injuries.

SAFETY SENSE

- You must participate in a complete warm-up and warm-down routine of flexibility exercises before and after games.
- You should have a good physical conditioning program that promotes endurance and speed training, knee muscle conditioning, and flexibility training.
- Make sure your training and coaching program accounts for the different types of playing surfaces. For example, you must learn proper techniques for sudden stops on

artificial surfaces to prevent toe injuries caused by jamming the foot into the end of the shoe.

- You must wear personal protection equipment, including shin guards, a mouth protector, and, if you are the goalie, face mask, pads, and gloves.
- Your shoes should not have metal cleats on the soles.
- You should not wear glasses, unless they are shatterproof or you use eye guards.
- Check your stick before each game or practice for splinters and cracks. Do not use it if it is damaged in any way.
- Check the field for holes, debris, and other obstacles.
- Make sure goal cages are brightly painted so you can see them easily and prevent a collision. If pipe or other metal is used for the cage, it should be padded.
- Make sure corner posts, goal lines, and center flagposts are made of plastic, not wood or metal.
- Always follow game rules. Most rules are written for your safety and protection.
- Make sure a medical attendant is present during match play.
- Encourage teams to wear contrasting uniform colors. The use of contrasting colors may help to prevent collisions between players on the same team, especially during split-second decisions.

Football (Flag/Touch)

RISK FACTORS
- No North American data are available. However, in one study at the college level, the touch football injury frequency rate was higher than in other intramural sports.

CONTRIBUTING FACTORS
- colliding with other players
- blocking or being blocked
- falls
- being hit by another player's elbow

COMMENT

From kids playing on pickup teams after school, to adults enjoying weekend exercise, more people are playing touch and flag football today than ever before. The opportunity for this limited-contact game is offered at schools, clubs, and recreational leagues for both males and females. In pickup games where younger players are pitted against older players and where field conditions are often poor and players do not always follow the rules, the potential for injury is particularly high. Supervised flag/touch football is a much safer sport.

SAFETY SENSE

- Wear sneakers (not cleats) and non-restrictive clothing. Remove objects, such as combs and pencils, from pants pockets.
- Invest in personal protection equipment, such as headgear, face guard, mouth piece, and elbow and knee pads.
- If you need corrective lenses, wear the kind designed for safety, with shatterproof lenses and safety frames. In addition, tape or pad the hinges and bridge.
- Make sure you are in good physical condition before playing and have a sufficient warm-up period before each game.
- Make sure the playing field is large enough, smooth, and free from obstacles. Don't get boundaries close to trees, fences, or park benches.
- Modify the rules to accommodate the size and ability of the players, and make sure all players understand and obey the rules.
- Learn the correct way to fall to prevent injury.

Football (Tackle)

RISK FACTORS
- It is estimated that over 350,000 people in North America are medically treated for injuries received while playing tackle football in organized and unorganized games.

CONTRIBUTING FACTORS
- blocking or tackling with your head down
- neck in flexed position
- hitting knees or thighs
- ramming your head into an opponent's chest
- being rammed by the opponent's helmet in your mid-section or back
- being struck in the head or neck with an extended forearm
- poorly maintained equipment

COMMENT

With thousands of schools, clubs, and other groups playing tackle football in North America, it is the primary responsibility of coaches to ensure that each player is provided with adequate protection against injuries and care for injuries that occur. Enforcement of safe practices and adherence to the rules of the game are very important in the prevention of injury.

SAFETY SENSE

Coaches
- Make sure every player has a medical examination and that the medical history is kept on record. Written permission from a physician must be presented to permit an injured player to return to the team, especially if a head injury was sustained.
- Make sure that players are in good physical condition. It is important to provide strength and endurance training, particularly for building up the neck muscles.
- When selecting equipment, deal with reputable equipment suppliers, buy the best equipment, make sure protective equipment is approved by standard-setting organizations, and ensure that old and worn equipment is discarded, not handed down to another player.
- During hot, humid weather, schedule practices in early morning or evening hours, provide lots of rest breaks and fluids, and monitor players carefully for heat stroke and exhaustion.
- Ensure that medical attendants are at each game and practice.

- A safe football program depends upon careful planning and organization by the coach. An attitude of "win at any cost" can lead to unnecessary injuries.
- Make sure playing fields are free of hazards, such as rocks, holes, glass, and other debris. There should be sufficient "run out" room at the ends of the field to prevent players from running into fences, walls, or bleachers. Ensure that goal posts are padded.
- Encourage teams to wear contrasting uniform colors. The use of contrasting colors may help to prevent collisions between players on the same team, especially during split-second decisions.

Players
- Do not strike an opponent with a fist, or deliver a blow with an extended forearm, elbow, palm, or heel.
- Do not kick or knee an opponent.
- Do not pile on or fall on an opponent after the ball is dead.
- Do not use a helmet deliberately to ram an opponent.

RISK FACTORS

- It is estimated that some 19 million North Americans play golf at least twice a year and that 0.12 percent of these golfers are treated annually for injuries at hospital emergency room centers.
- Golfers killed by lightning account for four percent of all lightning deaths in North America.
- Golf carts are involved in some 4,000 accidents each year in North America.

CONTRIBUTING FACTORS

- failing to get into reasonable physical condition before playing
- being struck by a golf ball or club
- being struck by lightning
- accident with a golf cart
- poorly maintained equipment

COMMENT

Golf is enjoyed by millions of people, and especially by seniors, who can enjoy the benefits of walking associated with golf. The common injuries that go unreported are muscle strains in the lower back, neck and shoulder, and golfer's elbow (soreness in elbow joints). Among recreational golfers, some injuries are attributed to poor technique and insufficient conditioning and warm-up. Others are a result of inconsiderate play.

SAFETY SENSE

- Begin pre-season flexibility exercises for the back, neck, and shoulders at least two weeks before your first visit to the course or driving range.
- If aches and pains continue while you are playing, you might wish to consult with a pro golfer or sports clinic to get an evaluation of your technique.
- Always stand away from and behind a player making a shot.
- Be aware of the flight patterns of balls being hit by other players when you are around the greens and alongside the fairways. This is especially important for spectators.
- Watch where you are walking; golf is played on uneven terrain.
- When playing a shot from a wrong fairway, ensure that the players playing that fairway are aware of your presence.

- Do not drink alcohol while golfing.
- Use sunscreen and on hot days drink lots of non-alcoholic fluids.
- During a thunderstorm, do not ride in golf carts or stay outdoors. Seek shelter in buildings, vehicles, or other locations that offer protection. If it is not possible to find a building, seek shelter in dense woods, depressed areas, small sheds, or tents. Avoid open fields, water areas, wire fences, railway tracks, overhead wires, isolated trees, and hilltops.
- Observe course rules concerning warnings to discontinue play. Generally, warnings consist of three consecutive notes of a horn. One prolonged note of a horn means resume play.
- If your golf club does not have lightning protection shelters on the course, encourage the management to erect them.
- Protect electric carts from lightning with a whip antenna of a length that will reach above the heads of the riders. The antenna acts as a lightning rod. Install a metal top or canopy. Steel-top automobiles are practically lightning proof.
- Drive carefully and slowly in golf carts. They are not toys.

Lacrosse

RISK FACTORS

- It is estimated that over 85,000 people in North America are treated medically for injuries received while playing lacrosse.
- In one college study, an injury rate of 52 percent was reported for lacrosse players, with most injuries occuring to the lower extremities.
- According to the same study, 90 percent of players do not wear mouth protectors.

CONTRIBUTING FACTORS

- being hit with the ball
- colliding with other players
- illegal acts and rule violations
- falls
- failing to wear protective equipment
- poorly maintained equipment

COMMENT

Lacrosse may appear to be a wild, free-swinging, injury-producing game; however, it can be a safe activity. With good officiating, protective equipment and clothing, and a good physical conditioning program, most injuries can be minimized.

SAFETY SENSE

- Make sure that you have a complete medical examination before starting the season.
- Wear protective clothing, including a helmet, face mask, gloves, mouth protector, and knee, arm, rib, and shoulder pads. Unsafe or worn-out equipment must be replaced immediately. You should also tape your wrist and ankles.
- When playing on grass, footwear should be of the soccer type. Football cleats often dig into the surface too much and cause strains and falls.
- If you are a coach, ensure that you teach the proper fundamentals of the game and that game rules are applied during practice.
- Ensure that players participate in a good physical conditioning program and do proper warm-ups before each game and practice session.
- Care must be taken to prevent heat exhaustion and fatigue during hot, humid weather. Take frequent rest breaks and drink plenty of fluids.
- Consider playing in a league that has modified the rules by restricting bodychecking or checking with the stick.
- If you are injured, make sure you have fully recovered before resuming play.
- Encourage teams to wear contrasting uniform colors. The use of contrasting colors may help to prevent collisions between players on the same team, especially during split-second decisions.

Polo

RISK FACTORS
- No North American data are available.

CONTRIBUTING FACTORS
- poor riding technique
- poor playing surface
- poor physical conditioning
- disregard for playing rules
- poorly maintained equipment

COMMENT

Polo demands a number of skills from its players. Polo players must learn to ride a horse and keep their balance while swinging the stick. But even if they have not had much riding experience, beginners soon find themselves improving. Most importantly, beginners should start the sport on a quiet animal, above all, on one that does not pull against the rider.

SAFETY SENSE

- Maintain a good physical conditioning program.
- You must wear a helmet with a chin strap that is securely tightened.
- Spend as much time as you can practicing how to stay on the horse and swing the stick. As a minimum, six months of polo experience should be obtained before going into a game.
- Learn how to position yourself on the field so that you keep active in the game, yet avoid bumping other players.
- Learn how to protect yourself if you are thrown off the horse. Stay put, curl up into a ball, and protect your head. Remember, other horses may be all around you.
- Have your horse checked regularly by a veterinarian. Horses are prone to injury, too, especially fetlock injuries.
- Keep your attention on the game at all times.
- Do not use a stick that whips or continuously swing the stick while galloping.
- Do not practice or tolerate fouling. Fouling is contrary to all the principles of fair play. By fouling, a player not only risks damage to himself and other players, but also to the horses.

- Fouls, such as "crossing" and "dangerous riding", are very serious. Players must understand how to avoid these hazardous situations.
- Never let your horse get out of control. Players who cannot control their mounts should be ejected from the game or should change mounts.
- Don't hit the ball haphazardly. It may hit an inattentive player.
- Encourage teams to wear contrasting uniform colors. The use of contrasting colors may help to prevent collisions between players on the same team, especially during split-second decisions.

RISK FACTORS
- No North American data are available.
- One U.S. study of college rodeo athletes estimated that there is an 89 percent chance of injury each season.
- In a study of U.S. professional athletes, bull riders accounted for 28 percent of all injuries, while saddle bronco and bareback riders accounted for 20 percent each.

CONTRIBUTING FACTORS
- falling from an animal
- being fallen on, stepped on, or kicked by an animal
- poorly maintained equipment
- extreme stress and impact on muscles and bones

COMMENT

Rodeo is a unique sporting event. Injuries are inevitable, because it is a physically unequal contest between the skills of a rider and the brute strength of an animal. A rodeo professional may participate in two or three rodeos a week, aggravating injuries that should have been given time to heal. The lack of on-site preventative care and education, which leads to inadequate self-treatment, is a major concern. Few people, however, view rodeo participants as athletes or the rodeo itself as a sport. Yet rodeos are popular in western colleges, and professional rodeo circuits are the main attraction to many western cities. In fact, there are more than 650 professionally sanctioned rodeos in North America.

SAFETY SENSE

- Unless you grow up on a farm or ranch, where the way of life teaches you the techniques you need to know, you should enroll in a school that teaches the different rodeo events.
- To get into shape, you should follow a rigorous physical conditioning program. Warm-up exercises before competitions help to reduce muscle strain.
- Wear protective hip, groin, and leg pads to protect against injury from an animal that falls or steps on you.
- Proper wrist taping and the use of elbow braces and forearm padding can help minimize injuries.
- It is advisable for steer wrestlers to wear mouthguard protection.
- It is advisable to wear head protection. Rodeo tradition makes helmet use unlikely at the professional level,

but its use should be mandatory at the college level.

- Chutes and gates should be padded.
- Check all equipment before each ride. Look for weakened saddle cinches, frayed ropes, and so on.
- When you are mounted within the chute, ensure that your feet and legs are up and forward of the animal's head so that you can dismount easily if the animal bolts up and over the gate before it is opened.
- Rodeo organizers must ensure that professional medical help is on site during competition.

Rugby

RISK FACTORS
- It is estimated that over 10,000 people in North America are medically treated for injuries received while playing rugby each year.
- In one Australian study, the injury rate for rugby was 198 injuries per 10,000 player hours, compared with 103 injuries in basketball and 27 injuries in field hockey.

CONTRIBUTING FACTORS
- improper tackling technique
- rule violations
- poor physical conditioning
- failing to consistently apply the crouch-touch-pause-engage (CTPE) rule for scrums
- insufficient pre-game warm ups

COMMENT

Rugby is played in many countries and is similar in some respects to North American football. However, in rugby, players do not use helmets, face masks, shoulder pads, or shin guards, and the game is kept in constant motion. Because of the lack of protective equipment, players are subject to a greater risk of injury if they are not playing with utmost concern for the rules.

SAFETY SENSE

- Ensure that players participate in good pre-season training and general conditioning programs. Good conditioning programs are particularly important since protective equipment is not used. Players need to develop specific muscle groups for playing certain positions. For example, props need to develop muscles in the neck and shoulder area.
- Wear a mouthguard to protect against teeth injuries.

- Tape ankles and wrists to help prevent sprains and strains.
- Never do a head-first tackle or violate any other rules. Coaches should bar from further play anyone who violate safety rules, including the CTPE rule.
- Enter all scrums, mauls, and rucks with your body in the correct alignment. Keep your shoulders higher than your hips, keep your head up to protect the neck from injury, and keep your eyes forward.

- If, during a scrum, maul, or ruck, you fall suddenly, start yelling immediately.
- Ensure that you have competent coaches and referees for games, to ensure player safety.
- Learn proper tackling techniques and practice these techniques frequently.
- If you are injured, seek medical attention immediately.
- Ensure that a physician is on site during all rugby matches.
- Make sure you have a sufficient supply of water to prevent heat exhaustion during play in hot, humid weather.
- Encourage teams to wear contrasting uniform colors. The use of contrasting colors may help to prevent collisions between players on the same team, especially during split-second decisions.

Soccer

RISK FACTORS

- It is estimated that over 100,000 people in North America are medically treated each year for injuries received while playing soccer.

CONTRIBUTING FACTORS

- rocks or holes in playing fields
- kicks
- poor playing skills
- incorrect footwear in poor weather conditions
- failing to brace neck when heading the ball
- colliding with other players
- poor physical conditioning
- poor officiating

COMMENT

Because soccer is a contact sport played with little or no equipment and because it puts great demands on stamina, numerous injuries occur. Estimates are that over nine million people play soccer in North America. While popularly thought to have originated in England, the game may well have been played in some form by the early Romans, who would have learned it from the Greeks.

SAFETY SENSE

- Participate in a good physical conditioning program and in mandatory warm-up exercises before games and practice sessions.
- Wear protective equipment, including shin guards and mouthguards. If you must wear corrective lenses, wear a protective guard over them.
- Wear standard soccer shoes, not football cleats. Studs must never be made of metal.
- If you are a goaltender, use protective equipment such as gloves; elbow, knee, and hip pads; and a warm-up suit during practice sessions to prevent abrasions and minor cuts.
- Encourage teams to wear contrasting uniform colors. The use of contrasting colors may help to prevent collisions between players on the same team, especially during split-second decisions.
- If you are injured, do not return to play until being examined by a physician.
- Examine the playing field for holes, rocks, and other debris before practices and games.
- Make sure goal posts are padded.

- Learn the safe method of heading a ball. Use your forehead so you can see the ball, tighten your neck muscles, and tuck your chin until the ball has been contacted; make sure your head is in line with your neck and trunk.
- If you are a goaltender, you must learn the correct way to dive and recover from falls.
- Do not play dangerously or violate rules. Coaches and referees must not tolerate such dangerous play.
- Ensure that all games are attended by a trained medical attendant.

Softball

RISK FACTORS
• No North American data are available.

CONTRIBUTING FACTORS
• being hit by the ball
• colliding with other players
• colliding with an obstacle on or near the field
• poor physical conditioning
• failing to warm up properly
• poorly maintained equipment

COMMENT

The game of softball has many forms: fast-pitch, slow-pitch, lobball, and many other variations are played in parks, streets, and open fields throughout the world. To minimize injury, you should consider the following basic safety sense.

SAFETY SENSE

• Take time before games to warm up in order to prevent common strains and muscle sprains.
• Use a softball glove for catching the ball to prevent finger and hand injuries.
• It is strongly recommended that batting helmets be worn, especially by young people and fast-pitch players.
• Catchers must wear face and head protection. In fast-pitch, the catcher should wear a chest protector, shin pads, and a groin protector.
• Make sure the playing field is free from debris, such as broken glass, potholes, rocks, and so on.
• Pitchers should follow through the pitch and be ready to field a ball hit back to them. Line drives can cause serious injury.
• Infielders should place one foot on the inside corner of the bag, giving most of the bag to the oncoming runner. This will prevent collisions and foot and ankle injuries.
• On fly balls, be aware of other fielders' positions and have a system for calling the ball to prevent collisions.
• Outfielders should be cautious of the fence. Smashing into it can cause a serious injury.
• Keep your eyes on the ball at all times and your mind on the game.
• Keep equipment and players well back from the playing field.

TRACK AND FIELD
AND GYMNASTICS

The popularity of track, field, and gymnastics events has contributed to an increase in the number of clubs and programs throughout North America.

Nothing is known of the first sport contest, but it may well have been a footrace. Today, one person racing another is still the simplest of all sports. Running, jumping, throwing, and feats of balance and strength attract the participation of both young adults and children. During the past few years, with the increase in injuries among participants, more attention has been given to accident prevention strategies. To this end, coaches are better trained; facilities and equipment must meet national safety specifications; and manufacturers of equipment have been made more aware of the safety requirements of these sports. They now consult with coaches, trainers, and competitors in order to eliminate flaws in safety mechanisms and construction of the equipment. Coaches are better trained, and facilities and equipment must meet national safety specifications.

Gymnastics

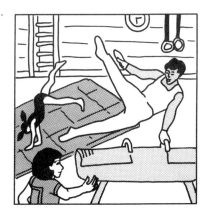

RISK FACTORS

- It is estimated that over 14,000 people are medically treated annually in North America for injuries received in gymnastics.
- In one study, injuries to competitive gymnasts occurred at a rate of 5 percent and to beginner gymnasts at a rate of 0.7 percent.

CONTRIBUTING FACTORS

- unsafe equipment (cracks on mats, spacing between mats, and so on)
- improper warm-up
- recklessness on equipment
- attempting skills beyond ability
- lack of or poor spotting
- improper instructions
- unsafe environment
- overexertion
- falls

COMMENT

Gymnastics has had a tremendous increase in popularity largely as a result of television exposure and the Olympics. The sport demands strength, balance, and body control. Paramount to preventing injuries is the need for a good physical conditioning program, well-maintained equipment and good instructions. Before taking up gymnastics, check with national gymnastic federations and local clubs for information on selecting a program. The safety sense information below deals with the basic safety requirements and does not address all the types of apparatus used.

SAFETY SENSE

- Do proper warm-ups; they should **not** include strengthening or fatiguing exercises.
- Wear appropriate clothing.
- Ensure that the instructor is providing competent supervision, instruction, discipline, and safe practices and is trained in first-aid.
- Make sure gymnastics areas are restricted to gymnastics only.
- Master the basic skills first and learn the elements of the skill before attempting to do it.
- Practice only when you are supervised.

- Appreciate the risk of each piece of equipment (e.g., falls from parallel bars) and always check the equipment before you use it.
- Clean chalk from the high bar, parallel bars, uneven bars, and rings to prevent wrist injuries.
- Wear properly fitted hand guards.
- Never purposely land on your head, neck, or back on any type of mat. No gymnastic mat is fail-safe in preventing injury.
- Ensure that equipment is properly maintained. It should be put away in a locked area after use; this is especially true of rebound apparatus, (spring boards, etc.).
- Make sure your workout schedule meets your particular needs and capabilities.
- Do not continue practicing when you are fatigued. Know your limitations.
- If you are a coach, do not attempt to teach skills for which performers are not ready.

Track and Field Events

RISK FACTORS
- It is estimated that nearly 50,000 people are medically treated in North America for injuries received while participating in track and field events.
- Most sprint and long distance running injuries occur during training.

CONTRIBUTING FACTORS
- sprains and strains
- improperly fitting footwear
- overexertion
- poor warm-up and warm-down procedures
- poor preparation of track surface or field event area
- lack of good physical conditioning
- improper techniques
- poor nutrition program
- collisions with equipment
- sudden increase in training intensity
- fatigue
- heat exhaustion
- struck by a motor vehicle during training

COMMENT

Track and field events grew out of the natural activities of primitive human beings. Running, throwing a spear (javelin), jumping over logs and ditches (high jump, long jump), and hurling stones (discus, shot put) are, some of today's popular track and field events.

Most young people who take part in track and field events are members of a school team or track club. Participation in a track and field event is a good means of physical conditioning.

SAFETY SENSE

- Have a medical examination before becoming involved in track and field events.
- Select good personal equipment for the event. Shoes should fit well and provide adequate support.
- Warm-up exercises should include jogging, stretching, and short sprints. Wear a jogging suit during your warm-up.
- When training, be aware of excessive workouts and your technique and speed. Injuries from overexertion often occur when athletes go beyond the training program recommended for them.
- Always warm down. Keep your jogging suit on for this activity, and slow your pulse rate back to normal before showering.
- When training for distance running in urban areas, be especially alert for motor vehicle traffic and, if training during evening hours, wear a retro-reflective safety vest.
- Ensure that jumping pits are well maintained and that runways are clear of debris.
- Ensure that the area used for throwing events (discus, javelin, shot put) are protected with cages and that the throwing field is clear of people. Never assume that others can see that you are training.
- Drink liquids before, during, and after workouts to prevent heat exhaustion. Avoid training during peak-temperature hours and in high humidity.
- Follow a schedule of rest and diet that meets the increased demands and stress placed on you by extensive practice and competition.
- If using work-out programs, such as weight training, be aware of injuries caused by overexertion and follow a program designed for your own abilities.
- If you receive an injury, no matter how minor, report it to your trainer or physician. If not treated properly, minor injuries can often result in problems later on.

Trampoline

RISK FACTORS

- A distinct decline in trampoline injuries has been observed since the late 1970s, mostly related to the banning of trampolines in schools and colleges. Most manufacturers have stopped selling the equipment and its replacement parts.
- Trampoline injuries to children aged 5 through 14 have accounted for 50 percent of all injuries treated at hospital emergency centers.
- Head and neck injuries account for an average of 20 percent of those reported injuries.

CONTRIBUTING FACTORS

- somersaulting
- failure to provide supervision and/or spotters
- recklessness
- failure to use safety harnesses during practice
- lack of skill and ability

COMMENT

Since the mid 1970s, the use of trampolines has created a major controversy between medical associations and trampoline enthusiasts. Medical associations argue that trampoline injuries cause too many quadriplegic injuries, while trampoline enthusiasts counter that life itself is filled with accidents. Since the late 1970s, there has been a decline in trampoline recreational facilities, and school physical education programs have discontinued instruction in the sport. Nevertheless, safety sense tips should be provided for those who use trampolines that are still accessible in parks, amusement areas, and clubs.

SAFETY SENSE

- Wear proper apparel, particularly nonslip footwear. If you jump barefoot, clean your feet and clip your toenails. It is advisable for beginners to cover elbows and knees with pads or clothing. Remove all jewelry, belts with buckles, and other potential hazards.

- You must learn the skills in the proper sequence, beginning with fundamental and leadup movements. It is up to an experienced instructor to determine when the basics are correct.
- Bounce only with permission and with supervision.

- Allow only one person on the trampoline at a time.
- Do not engage in wild horseplay.
- Do not bounce when fatigued, sleepy, on medication, upset, or distracted.
- Maintain an aggressive, confident attitude. Don't change your mind in mid air! More people are injured from being overly timid than from being overly aggressive.
- When learning new moves, stay low and in the center of the trampoline.
- Learn to do an effective "kill bounce" (an immediate stop from any height), and use it often, particularly when learning a new movement. If you have even the least suspicion that your landing isn't absolutely under control, kill bounce and fall on your back.
- Have an alternative strategy ready in case your landing is amiss. For example, if you're working to accomplish a belly landing but you realize you're going to land on your face, twist out to a back landing. If you're overthrowing a backward stunt, rotating towards your head, you must make an instant decision whether to tuck into a somersault (with an instant half twist out to back) or to throw your arms back behind your head and stop yourself.
- Ensure all trampolines are locked up and inaccessible when they are not supervised.
- Use safety devices, such as belts for spotting, with novice jumpers and during practice sessions.
- Outside of professional trampolining, it is advisable not to attempt to perform somersaults. All quadriplegic injuries seem to be a result of this maneuvre.

ATMOSPHERIC SPORTS

Flying is a challenge, but for those who accept it, the rewards can be great. There is a wide range of opportunities for those who want to discover the joys of flight. There is the rough-and-tumble of hang gliding, the high technology of soaring in a glider, the satisfaction of building and flying your own airplane, or the peaceful drifting flight of a balloon. If none of these is quite what you want, you can experiment quietly with human-powered aircraft at a height of 3 m (10 ft.) or dive from an airplane at 3,000 m (10,000 ft.), making patterns in the sky before opening your parachute.

The wide variety of flying sports now available means that there is something for practically everyone. Many people enjoy several such sports; after five years or so of exciting parachuting, for example, you may like to change gears and obtain a private pilot's license. Later, you may even find time to build an ultralight. This unit provides information on the safe aspects of these and many other flying sports. Enjoy the sky!

Gliders (Sailplanes)

RISK FACTORS
- No North American data are available.

CONTRIBUTING FACTORS
- weather conditions
- reckless behavior, such as "stunting"
- alcohol and drugs
- equipment failure
- failure to maintain safety devices

COMMENT

Gliders are winged, motorless aircraft that soar on the wind as silently and gracefully as birds. The goal of every glider flight is to soar as long as possible on rising air, known as "updrafts." Gliders can be launched from light aircraft or by wire launches or by towing with a ground vehicle. Each launch technique requires experienced towing personnel who understand the necessary safety procedures.

Glider pilots are regulated under federal aviation laws. Knowing the laws and following them can save your life.

SAFETY SENSE

- Never fly if you have been using alcohol or drugs.
- Avoid days when thunderstorms threaten. Some thunderheads are strong enough to suck a glider up inside the storm.
- When taking off from a winch or vehicle launch, keep the angle of climb limited so that a recovery from a cable break can be made at any time without stalling.
- Cable release hooks for a winch or vehicle launch should be of the type that will release easily even when side loads are on the hook. Some kinds of "safety" hooks tend to jam or require high forces to operate them when under side loads or fall tension.
- Check your release hook on every flight. The pair of rings that go into the release must be perfectly round. An elongated ring may wriggle around and lock itself above the spring-loaded automatic part of the release.

- Never use links of chain or non-standard rings for launching -- they may distort or jam.
- Make sure a "weak link" is placed within the tow system to protect the glider in case the load is too great, the winch or vehicle jerks the cable, or the pilot pulls the glider up too steeply during a fast launch. This "weak link" must be incorporated at the tow plane end of the rope. This will safeguard the glider, but will also ensure that if the rope becomes entangled during a landing it will break before it pulls the tail off the tow plane.
- All tow ropes must meet specific breaking strength requirements for the plane weight; always observe these ratings.
- Fasten a rope between the glider and the main cable to act as a shock absorber and to reduce vibration.
- Use a cable parachute to protect the launching cable. The parachute prevents the cable from falling too quickly after the release and becoming kinked or tangled.
- If you are launching from a winch or vehicle, be sure to have some sort of cable-cutting device on hand just in case the cable becomes tangled in the wheel or skid of the glider.
- Before an airplane launch, make sure that you have reviewed the procedures. Early training flights should be accompanied by an instructor.
- Never perform "stunts" unless you are an experienced stunt flyer.
- Never invert your glider while being towed.
- Do not make an unnecessarily low pass over an object.
- Make sure you have oxygen available if flying at a high altitude.

Hang Gliding

RISK FACTORS

- No North American data are available. However, it is estimated that about nine fatalities occur annually.

CONTRIBUTING FACTORS

- towing mishaps caused by inexperienced tow operators
- failure to have the nose-wire person tied in securely when assisting on cliff launches
- inexperienced wire assistants
- failure to hook in the glider's nose
- electrocution and electric shock from hydro lines
- landing accidentally in dangerous terrain (trees, rocks, water, etc.)

COMMENT

Hang gliders are the ancestors of modern sailplanes. In the 1970s, hang gliding as we know it today became a very popular sport. The typical glider is made of an aluminum frame over which synthetic fabric is stretched. The pilot straps himself or herself into a harness and launches the glider. This is typically done by running down a hill until reaching a speed fast enough to fly. The pilot controls the flight of the glider by pushing and pulling on a control bar and by shifting body weight to the left and right.

These small flying machines can be thrilling, but they require a great deal of skill and practice to manipulate safely. A hang glider offers little protection in case of a crash -- your caution must be your defense. Remember that the potential dangers in hang gliding increase with the wind velocity.

SAFETY SENSE

- Get good training before you attempt to use a hang glider. Join a local hang gliding club. You will need to learn many technical maneuvres and flight dynamics.
- Always yell "clear!" and check your clearance visually before taking off.
- In ridge-soaring conditions, crosswinds should not exceed 30°. In very light winds, a crosswind of up to 45° is acceptable.
- Exercise extreme caution during a widespread lift at greater than 150 m (500 ft.) per minute.

- Do not hang-glide when the gust factor is greater than ½ the mean velocity of the wind or when the wind speed changes more than 8 km/h (5 mph) in three seconds or less.
- Perform a hook-in check within 15 seconds of taking off. Check your attached carabiner (a steel or aluminum "O" shaped ring for ropes to slide through) and support straps.
- Stabilize in flight before climbing into your harness. Don't zip into a pod harness until you are 30 m (100 ft.) up or away from the hill.
- Stay two wing spans away from another glider in smooth conditions and five wing spans away in turbulence.
- Adjust your pitch until your velocity is steady and just above stall speed for efficient, coordinated turns.
- Check the space into which you will be moving to avoid mid-air collisions while turning.
- Whenever possible, avoid turning near the ground if the air is turbulent.
- Beginners should stay well clear of the ridge after launching.
- When riding a thermal over a mountain, stay within 45° (a one-to-one glide) of the front (upwind side) of the mountain.
- Never go over the back of a mountain with less than the height of the mountain over the top.
- Unzip a pod harness at 150 m (500 ft.). You should be over your landing field by then.
- Below 150 m (500 ft.), stay within 45°(a one-to-one glide) of your landing field. When obstructions surround the field, this 45° angle begins at 30 m (100 ft.) above the field boundaries.
- Below 30 m (100 ft.), increase your speed to 1½ times your stall speed plus ½ the wind speed.
- Stand up above 30 m (100 ft.) in open landing areas and above 10 m (30 ft.) in obstructed areas.
- Use a downwind for your final approach in winds below 24 km/h (15 mph).
- Flare to a no-step landing in most conditions. Note that flare timing is indicated by three items:
  - the velocity drops;
  - the control bar pressure changes; and
  - the glider settling.
- Vary the speed of a flare inversely with the speed of the glider when the flare begins.
- Never land downwind of an obstruction (hill, building, or trees) closer than the point where distance measured in multiples of obstruction heights equals the wind speed measured in kilometres per hour ($D=V$).

Hot Air Ballooning

RISK FACTORS
- On average, there are some 30 ballooning accidents a year in North America. About 15 percent result in a fatality.

CONTRIBUTING FACTORS
- flying balloons that are not airworthy
- pilot error during take-off or landing
- excessive winds blowing the craft off course into obstacles

COMMENT

Hot air ballooning, although invented in the late 1700s, did not become a popular sport until the 1960s when light nylon materials and compact tanks of pressurized propane gas became available. With the increasing interest in ballooning came government safety regulations. Balloons must be inspected and awarded a certificate of airworthiness before they are sold. Federal laws also regulate the number of occupants the balloon basket may carry, the strength of cables, and allowable construction materials. Balloonists must pass written tests dealing with meteorology.

If you wish to learn to operate a balloon, enroll in a training course. It generally takes about 16 hours to become certified and licensed.

SAFETY SENSE

- Thoroughly inspect the balloon before each flight.
- Before taking off, get weather forecasts for several altitudes at 1,000 foot increments; remember that wind is the only way to make the craft move.
- Carry extra propane tanks -- never take a chance of running out of fuel.
- Launch the craft in the early morning or late afternoon. The ground winds are more still at these times, and there will be less chance of losing control of the craft.

- If possible, choose a launch site with trees around its edge; these will protect you from ground wind.
- Always have a "chase vehicle" follow you for pick-up and in case of an emergency.
- Never fly while under the influence of alcohol; do not even carry alcohol on board.
- Before riding in a balloon as a passenger, check that the pilot holds a current license and/or that the balloon company is reputable. You may wish to check with your local federal aviation office.
- As much as possible, avoid flying in and around cities, airports, or large bodies of water.
- When landing, crouch down with your knees bent and face the direction of the landing. This will absorb some of the landing shock. If there is a handle, hang on to it.
- Land in open spaces, such as fields, but stay away from those with crops or animals in them.

- Always wear gloves to prevent rope burn.
- Be wary of thunderstorms. Follow these guidelines about thunderstorm conditions:
  - remember that vivid and frequent lightning means a severe thunderstorm is likely;
  - don't take off in the face of an approaching thunderstorm; a sudden gust front or low level turbulence could cause loss of control;
  - don't attempt to fly under a thunderstorm even if you can see through the other side; turbulence and windshear under the storm could be disastrous;
  - don't trust the visual appearance to be a reliable indicator of the turbulence inside a thunderstorm; and
  - avoid by at least 32 km (20 mi.) any thunderstorm identified as severe; this is especially important under a large cumulonimbus cloud formation.

Kite Flying

- No North American data are available.

CONTRIBUTING FACTORS

- electric shock or electrocution
- burns
- falls from high places (trees, poles, rooftops, etc.)
- motor vehicle accidents while flying kites on or near streets

COMMENT

The kite took its name from a bird of the hawk family, known for its powerful wings and gracefulness. Flying kites is a popular springtime sport and there are many kite competitions throughout North America. Although it is not usually considered a dangerous activity, accidents do happen during kite flying. Telephone and power companies report that the remains of thousands of kites are removed from lines annually.

SAFETY SENSE

- Fly your kite in a safe area. Never fly a kite near electrical wires or poles, streets and highways, railways, etc. Open level fields and parks are the best location.
- Fly your kite only in dry weather. A wet cord is a conductor of electricity.
- Do not use any metal in building a kite. Do not use wire or tinsel cord as a kite string.
- Never try to rescue a kite if it is caught on a wire or pole.
- Use reels and wear gloves when flying kites in strong winds; this will help prevent hand and finger burns.
- Don't run across rough or furrowed fields to launch your kite; the risk of a twisted ankle is high.

Model Airplanes and Rockets

RISK FACTORS

- No North American data are available. However, with the advent of inexpensive models and kits, injuries associated with model airplane flying and model rocketry are becoming more frequent because more people are participating in the activity.

CONTRIBUTING FACTORS

- burns from gasoline fires
- electrical shock and electrocution
- tampering with rocket engine fuel

COMMENT

Model airplane flying has been around since World War I. In the early days, the romance of air travel led many people of all ages into the hobby. As the space age began, so did a new enthusiasm for model rocketry. The Academy of Model Aeronautics (USA) and the Canadian Association of Rocketry can provide information on this sport. Use that information and some safety sense to pursue the hobby safely.

SAFETY SENSE

- Read the safety precautions listed in the unit on kite flying, page 158; many of these tips also apply to flying model planes and rockets.
- Fly your model away from power lines, trees, homes, pedestrians, and roadways. If there are spectators, keep them well back from danger. In some cases, this may require fences or supervision.
- Store flammable fuels very securely. Some of the fuels used for model airplanes will burn at temperatures as low at -6° C (20° F). Store fuel outdoors in metal containers with screw tops.
- Fuel planes out of doors, **never** in confined places.
- Keep only a small amount of fuel on hand. By law, a rocket engine may not contain more than 125 grams (4.4 oz.) of low explosive fuel. If any fuel is spilled on the engine wipe it off immediatly before it can catch fire.
- Follow manufacturers' recommendations regarding strength of wire, proper grounding, etc.

- Choose a clear day for launching a rocket -- visibility should be greater than 500 m (1,600 ft.). Also choose a day with winds less than 35 km/h (20 mph). Most rockets descend with a parachute, so a strong wind can blow them way off course.
- Do not allow young children to fly or launch rockets unsupervised. In some jurisdictions, you may need a license and be of a certain age to purchase a rocket engine.
- Store rocket engines in a dry, cool area, away from small children.
- Never expose a rocket engine to temperature in excess of 65° C (149° F) or to open flames.
- Never play with, alter, or extract the fuel from a rocket engine.

Sky Diving (Parachuting)

RISK FACTORS
- Based on a five-year average, it is estimated that 43 parachuting fatalities occur annually in North America. Of this number, 31 percent are students, 45 percent are intermediate jumpers, and 24 percent are experts.
- Over 80 percent of all parachuting injuries occur during landing.

CONTRIBUTING FACTORS
- nonstandard progressions
- borrowed gear and inadequate transition
- jumping near water without floatation equipment
- chute failure
- jumper error (losing track of time and altitude leading to "lowpull")
- improper landing

COMMENT

Parachuting goes back to the 1700s when people used primitive parachutes to jump out of balloons and off towers. The first airplane jump was made in 1912. The modern sport of parachuting (sky diving) really got started in the 1950s. Today there are an estimated 400,000 jumpers worldwide.

Sky diving has its risks, however, and it is not for everyone. If you are a beginner, check out local clubs and instructors to determine if the sport is for you.

SAFETY SENSE

- Always check your basic jumping equipment: main chute, a reserve chute on the chest or back, helmet, goggles, overalls, and boots.
- Before you jump, be sure you have understood how to land properly. This is paramount in preventing injury -- a correct landing distributes the impact throughout your entire body.
- Recover quickly from the landing and collapse the chute fully to avoid being dragged by wind gusts.
- Make sure that there is ample space between you and other jumpers before releasing the chute -- otherwise you may become entangled with another chute.
- While learning, make sure that your instructor provides you with a one-way radio speaker so that you can receive instructions during the jump.

Ultralight Airplanes

RISK FACTORS

- It is estimated that there are some 460 ultralight airplane accidents annually in North America. As a result of these accidents, approximately 60 people die.

CONTRIBUTING FACTORS

- frostbite during winter flights
- hypothermia
- pilot error
- equipment failure

COMMENT

Anyone interested in ultralight flying should take a course, as you would need to do for any other aircraft. You will learn about meteorology, air laws, pilot navigation, and principles of flight. You must thoroughly understand federal aviation regulations pertaining to ultralight vehicles before trying to fly one, and you must be licensed.

SAFETY SENSE

- Do a thorough maintenance check and inspection prior to every flight.
- Check current weather forecasts before taking off and watch weather conditions while flying.
- Avoid alcohol and drugs before flying, at least 24 hours prior to takeoff.
- Never try to fly an overloaded ultralight.
- While taxiing out, take note of any objects that might present a hazard.
- Observe safety precautions when refuelling (don't smoke, clean up spills).

- Wear an inflatable life jacket (PFD) if you will be flying over water.
- Never fly when you are overtired.
- Remember that night comes on the surface of the earth sooner than it does at higher altitudes. Landing could present a problem if you stay up past dusk.
- If flying in winter, follow these additional safety rules:
  - wear specialized winter clothing for both safety and comfort: clothes should have a maximum of insulation, a minimum of bulk, and an

outer layer that is as impermeable to wind as possible;
- protect your head and face from heat loss. Do not use a scarf -- it could come loose and get into the propeller. If you wear a face shield, it should be treated with anti-fog solution and designed so that it swings out easily;
- protect hands with ski gloves or with mittens, which are warmer than finger gloves. Whatever you choose, make sure you can operate all instruments and controls;
- use boots, such as snowmobiler's foam-insulated boots, for foot protection;
- if you get cold enough that you begin to shiver, you are in danger; land at once;
- if the weather is very cold, you may need some sort of heating device to prevent icing in the carburator;
- check all working parts -- things, such as nylon bearings, may become too stiff or too loose and some parts may crack in extreme cold; and
- replace oil and grease with lighter oils before winter flying, since cold weather makes oil and grease thicken.

FIGHTING SPORTS

People have always fought with each other. The first men and women probably battled with sticks and stones over a piece of ground or the carcass of a dead animal. As time passed, we invented weapons of war. Flint axes and wooden spears gave way to metal swords and metal spears. Armies clashed on horseback or on foot, killing thousands.

Some warriors developed great skill in the use of weapons. The best fighters often became trainers, teaching others art of war. In this way, fighting skills were taken from the battlefield. In many societies, competitions of battle skills were used in the training of young men. Greek youth wrestled and boxed as part of their preparations for war. The Romans threw javelins. The Vikings used bows and arrows. Chiefs of tribes and leaders of nations encouraged their followers to take part in these fighting sports to keep fit and be ready for combat at short notice.

With the passing of time, conditions became more settled and peace more frequent. The energies of young people were needed less for fighting, and the training became an end in itself. So the various fighting sports that we know today gradually appeared. Such tests of skill and strength as boxing, wrestling, and the martial arts grew and changed until they became popular modern sports, many of them practiced throughout the world.

Boxing

RISK FACTORS
- It is estimated that over 5,000 people in North America are treated for boxing injuries each year.
- Nine percent of all boxing injuries occur to the face, mouth, eye, and ear.
- Hand injuries account for nearly five percent of all boxing injuries.
- Head injuries account for less than two percent of all injuries.

CONTRIBUTING FACTORS
- lack of good physical conditioning
- poor training technique
- mismatched weight
- failure to wear or maintain protective equipment
- carelessness

COMMENT

To some people, boxing is a brutal sport; while to others, it is the ultimate challenge in skill and strength. While the sport has its element of risk, it is very well regulated at both the professional and amateur levels.

All boxers, from novices to highly experienced fighters, should participate in a boxing club where the sport is properly supervised. Never encourage children, youths, or adults to purchase boxing gloves and "go at it" at home. Too often, injuries result from a mismatch of boxers' size, strength, and skill.

SAFETY SENSE

- Always use protective equipment. This includes properly padded headgear, mouthguard, athletic support (cup), high-top shoes, properly weighted gloves, and wrapped bare hands.
- Never box in a ring unless it is properly maintained. Above all, the floor should be constantly checked for moisture, especially during competition; a wet floor will cause slips and falls.
- Do not take up the sport without a general medical examination.
- Have regular medical examinations after participating in a competitive event.
- Ensure your club has trained referees who enforce the rules of the sport.
- Obtain and read a copy of the "safety code," available from a boxing federation. This code outlines in detail the specific safety precautions and medical aspects of this strictly regulated sport.

Exercise Equipment

RISK FACTORS

- It is estimated that some 20,000 people in North America are treated each year for injuries received while working with exercise equipment.

CONTRIBUTING FACTORS

- failure to follow operating instructions
- ignoring safety precautions
- overexertion
- children left unattended around equipment

COMMENT

You may want to consult a professional exercise physiologist or sports medicine doctor before buying exercise equipment. An expert can give individualized evaluations and offer advice on how to use equipment and which pieces to use to meet your specific needs. The YMCA/YWCA also trains experts who are qualified to evaluate your muscular strength, cardiovascular fitness, flexibility, and lean body weight.

Pay attention to what you are getting for your money. You may not want to pay for an expensive model that has an ergometer and a sleek design that is nice, but not necessary. On the other hand, you don't want to buy a model that is cheaply made and apt to break down.

If you buy safe equipment and then use it correctly, you can ensure that your equipment will build you up and not break down.

SAFETY SENSE

- If buying equipment for home use, make sure you have room -- preferably in a place with good ventilation since you will be working up a sweat.

- Test out equipment in the store whenever possible. How smoothly does it operate? Can you safely and easily change the machine from one exercise function to another? Is it sturdy, or does it shift on the floor or shake when used at maximum resistance or speed?

- Be especially cautious when purchasing an exercise device through the mail, since you can't examine it beforehand. Check the company's return policy in case you are not satisfied with the equipment.
- Look for heavy tubular steel and strong bolts, rather than thin screws and pins. If the equipment is electrical, it should carry a marker from Underwriters' Laboratories, Canadian Standards Association, American Society of Testing and Materials, or another recognized testing laboratory.
- Check that moving parts, such as chains on exercise bicycles, are guarded. Look for strong steel or coated cables rather than bare nylon or fabric, which may eventually fray.
- Before buying, read the operating manual and ask the salesperson to point out potential hazards. Even well-built equipment can be unsafe if used improperly; always follow manufacturers' recommendations for safe operation.
- On hard floors, use a thick mat to protect your back.
- If installing equipment in the home, consider what safety features are needed to protect your family. If there are disabled people or young children in the family, look for built-in safety guards and be prepared to supervise and properly store the equipment at all times.
- Store rowing machines in an upright position when not in use. Because the seat glides easily back and forth, children may see it as a plaything, and perhaps fall off or pinch their fingers.
- Watch out for collars on free weights that can loosen up during use, sending the weights crashing to the floor.
- Repair or replace parts on any device that needs maintenance to avoid hazards that come with wear such as loose bolts, springs, and handles. Remember: your body becomes stronger with use, but your exercise equipment does not!

Martial Arts

RISK FACTORS

- It is estimated that over 18,000 people each year in North America are treated for injuries received while participating in a martial art sport (judo, karate, kung fu, etc.).
- Sixty percent of the victims are between the ages of five and 24.

CONTRIBUTING FACTORS

- uncertified instructors
- undue emphasis on discipline and endurance instead of skill and technique training
- failure to wear protective equipment
- incorrect falling and throwing techniques
- recklessness
- loss of control
- unsupervised practice and training sessions
- injury from attack weapons (e.g., knives)

COMMENT

A wide variety of martial arts are practiced as sports today: karate, judo, tae kwon do, tai chi chuan, jujitsu, aikido, and more. This unit will present only the safety sense information required for the safe practice of the two most popular styles, karate and judo. Others exist that involve weapons, such as chains, nunchaku (two sticks connected by a cord or chain), and throwing stars, but the author does not believe it is appropriate to promote martial arts involving weapons.

SAFETY SENSE

- Wear protective equipment. At a minimum, this should include mouthguard, groin cup, breast cups, gloves, kick boots, and head protection. Forearm, shin, knee, and elbow pads are recommended.
- Select a qualified instructor. Check around and ask other people about various instructors. Are they certified? What is their philosophy on self-defense? Talk with them or observe a class in session. Do they have first-aid certification?
- Insist on careful, exacting, and controlled instruction; this will greatly reduce the number of injuries.
- Never exert pressure to an opponent's knees, ankles, or other joint.
- Always train on mats.

- Spar with a partner who is your match in experience and weight.
- Keep classes small enough that proper supervision is possible.
- Master falling skills first of all -- they are the most important. Fear of falling is not only a serious safety hazard, but the fear undermines all aspects of throwing offense and defense.

War Games

RISK FACTORS
- No North American data are available.

CONTRIBUTING FACTORS
- hit in the head, face, or eye with a paint pellet
- reckless play
- poor handling of a weapon
- equipment malfunction
- falls

COMMENT

In recent years, a new kind of combat game called a war game or adventure game has become popular. It is played by two teams in a wooded area, with each team trying to capture the other team's flag. Players are armed with CO_2 guns that shoot paint pellets. You "kill" opponents by firing paint pellets at them; a player splashed with paint is "wounded" or "dead."

The main hazards of this game seem to result from the players' total involvement in a simulated war. They run, jump, hide, climb trees, and do just about anything to avoid being shot. People can get so carried away that they do very dangerous things; only mature adults should consider playing these games.

These games are not for people who have had no formal instruction on the safe operation of a weapon (gun, pistol, etc.).

SAFETY SENSE

- Always wear protective eye goggles while in or near the playing area.
- Never participate if you or others in the group have been drinking alcohol.
- Do not smoke when in the playing area; smoking may cause accidental fires.
- People standing or waiting in the "free zone" (an area where a player stays if shot) must keep their weapons unloaded and safely secured. Better yet, store weapons outside of the "free zone."
- Before participating in such games, be sure to read the liability agreement form that must be signed by all players.

Weight Lifting and Body Building

RISK FACTORS

- It is estimated that some 74,000 people each year in North America are treated for injuries received while lifting weights or using exercise equipment.

CONTRIBUTING FACTORS

- suffocation
- fainting due to improper breathing
- failure to use safety devices on equipment
- improper lifting techniques
- lifting without "spotters"
- poor maintenance of equipment

COMMENT

Many athletes seem to subscribe to the philosophy that "more is better." This is why so many athletes end up suffering from the symptoms of overtraining. If you follow a training program that is too strenuous, in time, your body will completely lose the ability to recuperate and serious injuries can result. Therefore, it is important to establish a reasonable program that allows the body time to rest.

SAFETY SENSE

- If you are a serious body builder, or if you are over 40 years old and lift weights, you should have a thorough physical examination.
- Always warm up sufficiently before lifting.
- Work with a competent teacher who will base your training program on proven physiological and kinesiological principles to avoid overtraining and injury, as well as to gain optimal results.

- To avoid soreness, allow your muscles to adjust gradually to the workload.
- Perform all lifts correctly to prevent undue strain on joints.
- Be sure you have enough space; a crowded area can increase the risk of accidents. In a standard gym, several areas each 3 m (10 ft.) square should be marked off for training, and only the lifter and spotters permitted in these areas.

- Use spotters to help prevent injury while lifting. Always work with a buddy.
- Be sure that collars on barbells and dumbbells are firmly secured. Otherwise, if a barbell or dumbbell is not perfectly horizontal to the ground, the plates may slide off the bar and possibly injure the lifter and/or spotters.
- Determine the proper amount of weight to be lifted in each exercise, the number of repetitions and sets, and the precise time when additional weights should be added only with the help of a qualified training supervisor.
- Use only well-constructed training equipment; maintain it properly and inspect it regularly for unsafe features.
- Inhale to begin a lift and exhale before completing it; holding your breath throughout could cause you to faint and fall.
- Do not bounce the weight off your chest; this could cause chest, lung, and/or heart damage.
- Do not jerk the weight; this could lead to back and shoulder injury.
- See page 166 for safety sense information on selecting exercise equipment.

Weight Lifting and Children

RISK FACTORS
- Half of the estimated 44,000 weight-lifting injuries treated in North American hospital emergency rooms last year happened to children 10 to 19 years old.

CONTRIBUTING FACTORS
- lifting too much weight
- equipment falling on someone
- lack of supervision

COMMENT

Not so long ago, body builders and Olympic weight lifters were just about the only people doing presses and curls. But today, many teenagers and even young children work out with weights. Although most weight-lifting injuries are only minor sprains and strains, many parents are concerned enough to ask questions about the safety and benefits of weight lifting for their sons and daughters.

Physicians see little value for youngsters in weight lifting. Hoisting the maximum amount of weight in a single lift is a goal for Olympic competitors; when a child tries it, the result is frequently an injury.

Even weight training may not be of much value to pre-adolescent boys. Testosterone, the male hormone that enables muscle size to increase, is not present in levels that would increase muscle mass in boys who have not reached puberty. Some physicians are concerned that young children who often lift too-heavy weights may suffer injuries to developing bones.

Yet most experts feel that, although the benefits will be minimal, no harm will come to a child who works out with light weights under supervision and proper instruction. The best advice for a youngster interested in working out with weights is to get some help from an experienced trainer and don't overdo.

SAFETY SENSE

- Be sure youngsters work out only under supervision and instruction. A child lifting weights at home without guidance is likely to put too much weight on a bar and get hurt.
- Teach youngsters to start with light weights and work up slowly. Even when they go to a gym for instruction, children tend to be overenthusiastic when they begin working with weights and may suffer injuries as a result.
- Be sure young lifters who work out at home have spotters to lend a hand if they do lift too much. Weight lifters have died when a barbell that turned out to be too much to handle landed on the lifter's throat or chest.
- Remember that even if at-home lifters are conscientious about safety and keep the weights light, they may not benefit much from workouts if they don't follow programs that exercise all muscles. Working on one set of muscles and ignoring others sets a young athlete up for potential injuries in unexercised areas.

RISK FACTORS

- It is estimated that over 40,000 people each year in North America are treated for injuries received while wrestling.
- In one six-year study of U.S. high schools, it was reported that sprains accounted for 36 percent of wrestling injuries, contusions for 28 percent, strains for 23 percent, dislocations for 5 percent, fractures for 5 percent, and concussions for 3 percent.

CONTRIBUTING FACTORS

- spiking opponent
- falls
- throwing and slamming opponent onto head, neck, or shoulders
- lack of protective equipment
- poorly maintained mat surfaces
- poorly trained referees
- incorrect lifting procedures
- poor physical conditioning and dietary habits

COMMENT

Wrestling -- not the kind you see on television, which involves more costume and hype than actual strength and skill, but the "real" kind commonly referred to as "amateur wrestling" -- is a sport where great skill, strength, and speed are used to pin an opponent's shoulders down to the ground or to a mat. There are various forms, including freestyle, Greco-Roman, and sambo. If you or your children want to get involved in the sport, contact an amateur wrestling association, federation, athletic union, or club.

SAFETY SENSE

- Ensure that old injuries are rehabilitated properly to prevent repeat injuries.
- Aways have a physician and/or athletic trainer attend a competitive match.
- Use enough mats to provide cushioning even if a wrestler is taken out-of-bounds and thrown.
- Always wear proper head gear and protective padding during practice and competition.

- Before a match or practice session, warm up. A slight sweat is usually a good sign that you are sufficiently warmed up.
- To prevent muscle and fatigue-related injuries, wrestle only when following a program of physical conditioning.
- Be sure coaches provide adequate supervision. Often during practice, wrestlers get injured as a result of horseplay or accidental collision with others.
- Wrestle someone of your own weight and experience during both competition and practice.
- Watch out for too much weight loss (this is a common problem for wrestlers who want to stay in a specific weight class). Excessive dieting can lead to fainting and injury.
- Always have a pre-match and annual medical examination.
- Ensure that you are receiving good instruction on wrestling techniques and rules from a qualified coach or trainer.
- Novice wrestlers should not enter into competition until they can demonstrate proper wrestling skills.

ARTS AND CRAFTS*

An amateur photographer who worked in her darkroom on weekends suddenly found she had red rashes all over her hands. Because she had had no problems in the past, she didn't connect the symptoms with her hobby. Then she read about the hazards of darkroom chemicals in a photography magazine and realized the rashes might be linked to photographic developers. When she started using rubber gloves and tongs, the rashes disappeared.

People often do not realize that they may be at risk from their hobbies. Yet, many people involved in arts and crafts are exposed to substances that can cause health problems such as the ones in this example. Many commonly-used craft materials and processes are not as harmless as they seem. Whether you work with wood, glass, metal, clay, ink, or some other substance, you should be aware of the potential hazards and do what you can to reduce them. One important step is to get the facts about any chemicals you use in your craft work. Ask at your public library for reference works or contact a craft guild that gives detailed information about such substances and their hazards. In the United States, contact:

> Center for Safety in the Arts
> 5 Beekman Street
> New York, New York   10038
> (212) 227-6220.

The Center also publishes the Art Hazards News, a four-page newsletter appearing ten times per year and covering such topics as new hazards, precautions, etc. In Canada, contact:

> Ontario Crafts Council
> Resource Centre
> 346 Dundas Street West
> Toronto, Ontario   M5T 1G5
> (416) 977-3551.

NOTE: There is no statistical data available in North America that conclusively attributes a certain number of deaths to home arts and craft activities. However, there is evidence that toxic art materials can be a real danger to long-term health. In 1981, the U.S. National Cancer Institute surveyed 1,598 artists and reported that "artists who had a lifetime of exposure to pigments and solvents had significantly elevated risks of contracting heart disease, leukemia, and cancers of the bladder, colon, rectum, kidney, and brain."

---

*Some material in this unit is reproduced with permission of the Minister of Supply and Services Canada.

Clays, Plasters, Wax, Stone Carving, and Plastics

RISK FACTORS
- No North American data are available.

CONTRIBUTING FACTORS
- improper handling of raw materials
- inhalation of fumes and gases
- exposure to hazardous materials (pigments, varnishes, lacquers)

COMMENT

When working with clay, the main danger is inhaling dusts, powders, toxic gases, and fumes. Cancer and asbestosis may result from inhaling talc, which is found in many low-fire and slip-casting clays. Powdered clay can release large quantities of crystalline silica, which may cause silicosis.

The principal ingredient of plaster is calcium sulphate, a mild lung irritant which, along with other additives, may cause skin or respiratory problems. When used for hand or face molds, hardening plaster can also cause serious burns.

Overheating wax creates flammable vapors and strong lung irritants. Hydrocarbon solvents, such as carbon tetrachloride, are extremely hazardous and can be fatal.

Carving soft stones can present dust inhalation problems, particularly with soapstone (silica, asbestos) and sandstone (silica). Silica is also a problem when working with granite and many gemstones. Machine tools create more dust than hand tools and increase the risk of flying particles. Pneumatic tools can cause hearing loss and "white fingers" -- a vibration-related numbness that can lead to permanent damage of the circulatory system.

Working with plastic resins is extremely hazardous. Polyester (fiberglass), epoxy, acrylic, polyurethane, amino and formaldehyde resins and their hardeners, catalysts, and other additives can cause severe skin and respiration problems. Many are highly flammable. Heating, sawing, and sanding finished plastics can cause them to decompose into toxic substances: for example, polyurethane forms hydrogen cyanide.

SAFETY SENSE

- Learn from a crafts guild about the hazards of the materials and processes you use.
- Avoid processes involving plastics or dusts when working with children.
- Never eat, drink, or smoke in the work area. Wash your hands and arms thoroughly before eating or preparing food.
- Wear special work clothes and wash them separately from other laundry.
- Wet-mop or wet-vacuum all surfaces daily; sweeping stirs up dusts.
- If you are pregnant, avoid products containing plastic resins and solvents.
- Be sure you have good ventilation; this means canopy hoods for kilns and specialized local exhaust ventilation for plastic resins.
- Use a respirator as a last resort. Be sure that it is approved by the National Institute of Occupational Safety and Health (NIOSH) for the substance you are using.
- When working with stone, plaster, or clay, avoid asbestos-contaminated material.
- Never use an open flame to heat wax, and never overheat it. Use varsol or naphtha to replace carbon tetrachloride. Avoid chlorinated synthetic waxes.
- Use pneumatic and electric tools with portable dust collectors. Prevent "white fingers" by taking frequent work breaks, keeping hands warm, and using comfortable handgrips. Isolate noisy compressors.
- Wear protective equipment, such as goggles and a face shield, face mask, eye and hearing protectors, and non-asbestos gloves.
- Maintain machinery according to the manufacturer's instructions; inspect it regularly for electrical hazards.
- Keep long hair, clothing, and jewelry away from moving parts.

Glass Blowing

RISK FACTORS

- No North American data are available.

CONTRIBUTING FACTORS

- heat stress
- failing to wear eye protection
- carbon monoxide poisoning
- metal poisoning
- burns from acid, thermal, and infrared sources

COMMENT

Many chemicals used to make glass are highly toxic, including lead, arsenic, and silica and its compounds. Furnaces for making glass present additional hazards, including poisonous carbon monoxide gas; infrared radiation, which can cause cataracts; and intense heat, which poses the risk of heatstroke.

When working freeblown glass, the risk of physical accidents is great: heavy gathers of glass are swung at the end of long pipes in an atmosphere of intense heat. This is also the most difficult stage at which to dispel the fumes, vapors, and toxic gases that form when colorants or other chemicals are added.

Coloring and decorating hazards depend on the processes and chemicals used. Fuming techniques, in particular, can create serious inhalation problems. Hydrofluoric acid and fluoride-salt etching can cause serious burns. Abrasive blasting with sand can produce silicosis, and the noise can cause hearing loss.

When working with stained glass, lead is the most serious hazard. It can be inhaled or ingested while soldering or sanding, or while applying lead-based pigments. Both lead-came and copper-foil techniques produce lead fumes, but copper-foil is more hazardous because higher temperatures are required.

Soldering fluxes produce fumes when heated. Many, such as zinc chloride, are severe lung irritants. Inhaling rosin fluxes can lead to asthma.

SAFETY SENSE

- Learn from a crafts guild about the hazards of the materials and processes you use.
- Never allow young children in the work area.
- Never eat, drink, or smoke in the work area. Wash your hands and arms thoroughly before eating or preparing food.
- Wear special work clothes and wash them separately from other laundry.
- Wet-mop or wet-vacuum all surfaces daily; sweeping stirs up dusts.
- If you are pregnant, avoid using products containing lead or powdered pigments.
- If you have heart or kidney problems, check with your doctor before risking the high temperatures glass blowing requires.
- Wear protective equipment: infrared goggles and non-asbestos gloves when glass blowing; acid-proof goggles and clothing when etching; and hearing protectors for abrasive blasting (outside an enclosed cabinet, use special respiratory protection as well).
- Use cullet or prepared glass whenever possible to avoid the chemical hazards of making glass.
- Use fluoride pastes instead of more hazardous hydrofluoric acid when etching.
- When blasting with abrasives, substitute glass beads, aluminum oxide, or silicon carbide (carborundum) for sand. If working indoors, always use an enclosed blasting cabinet.
- Ensure good ventilation. Gas-fired furnaces must be vented, preferably with a canopy hood. Solder stained glass directly in front of a window equipped with an exhaust fan, or use a slot hood. For etching and fuming, use a fume hood.
- Use a respirator as a last resort. Be sure it is approved by the National Institute of Occupational Safety and Health (NIOSH) for the substance you are using.

Lapidary Arts

RISK FACTORS
- No North American data are available.

CONTRIBUTING FACTORS
- cuts
- flying particles of rock
- inhaling fine rock dust
- vibration from machines causing finger and hand numbness

COMMENT

Lapidary art is very satisfying, especially if you are interested in designing and making jewelry. Polished rocks that are sized and shaped can also be used in many other items, such as lamp bases, decorative plaques, and just about anything else you can think of. Just keep in mind the proper safety sense when using lapidary tools and equipment.

SAFETY SENSE

- Wear impact/dust goggles when shaping or chipping materials.
- Wear steel-tipped shoes when working with heavy materials or equipment.
- Follow correct lifting and carrying procedures when you move heavy stones and other objects.
- Use electric grinding and polishing tools that are equipped with local exhaust connections for removing dust from the studio. Clean up after each work session in order to control other sources of dust.
- If you need respiratory protection, match the respirator filters to the type of dust produced. Do not expect air-purifying respirators to filter heavy amounts of dust. For high dust levels, you may need an air-supplied respirator.
- Purchase quiet tools and exhaust fans, or wear hearing protection.
- When using electric tools, take frequent rest breaks to prevent "white fingers."

Leather

RISK FACTORS
- No North American data are available.

CONTRIBUTING FACTORS
- inhaling toxic substances
- ingesting toxic substances
- lack of protective equipment and clothing
- fire
- poor ventilation in the work area
- cuts and stabs

COMMENT

Working with leather can involve a wide variety of processes, from cutting to carving, sewing, cementing, dyeing, and finishing the leather. Visit any craft show and you will soon realize that leather working can, for a talented crafts person, create beautiful items and perhaps provide extra income. It can also be an enjoyable activity, and it is relatively inexpensive to get started. However, the craft does have some serious health and safety hazards.

Inhalation of leather dust results in increased rates of nasal cavity, sinus, and bladder cancer among leather and shoe workers. However, this appears after 40 to 50 years of exposure, and is probably not a serious hazard for recreational leather craftpersons.

Products used in cementing, dyeing, and finishing can be hazardous. For example, rubber cements and their thinners are labelled "extremely flammable" and usually contain hexane, which is highly toxic if inhaled.

SAFETY SENSE

- Wear an approved face mask to protect against inhaling dust.
- Do not allow leather dust to accumulate. Vacuum it regularly and wet-mop. Work outside or have an exhaust ventilation installed.
- When using cutting tools, cut in a direction away from you, and keep your free hand behind or to the side of knives and other tools that can slip.

- Never try to catch a sharp tool that falls.
- Read the instructions on the materials to be used and follow directions.
- Use leather dyes that contain ethyl alcohol rather than orthodichlorobenzene or monochlorotoluene.
- Wear rubber-based gloves when using solvents and dyes.
- Use solvents only when good general ventilation is provided. Do not operate heating or air conditioning systems when working with leather. This only spreads the contaminants throughout the home or studio.
- Do not smoke or have open flames in areas where solvents are used.
- Store waste rags in a self-closing safety container.
- Wash your hands thoroughly before eating.

Metal Work

- No North American data are available.

CONTRIBUTING FACTORS

- exposure to infrared and ultraviolet radiation
- burns from molten metal, electric arc, or solder
- inhaling of metal fumes and gases
- electrical shock

COMMENT

Working with metal -- whether welding, soldering, or molding -- can be extremely hazardous. Attempt it only if you are properly trained and have correct safety equipment.

Metal fumes are a serious danger. Galvanized metals and zinc or copper alloys can cause metal-fume fever, which has symptoms much like the flu. Cadmium fumes can cause chemical pneumonia, as well as lung and kidney damage.

Welding creates large amounts of infrared and ultraviolet light, which can cause skin cancer, severe sunburn, and eye damage. Arc welding produces nitrogen dioxide and ozone, both severe lung irritants that can cause immediate chemical pneumonia and long-term lung damage. The compressed gases used in oxyacetylene welding could cause fire and explosions. Other welding hazards include burns and electrical shock.

Other dangers of working with metal include inhaling dusts, fumes and gas, as well as heat, noise, and infrared radiation. For example, many products used for molds can produce enough dust to cause silicosis. Resin-casting sands are usually based on formaldehyde, a highly toxic irritant of skin and the respiratory tract. Lacquers, especially when sprayed, can induce acute narcosis and possible chronic damage to nerves, liver, and kidneys. Buffing, polishing, and grinding, in addition to obvious mechanical hazards, can produce particles and dusts harmful to the eyes and respiratory system.

Soldering can expose you to the risk of being burned from the heat or solder paste, which is an acid, and the potential of lead poisoning, which can cause damage to kidneys and lungs.

SAFETY SENSE

- Learn from a local crafts guild about the hazards of the materials and processes you use.
- Keep young children away from the work area.
- Never eat, drink, or smoke in the work area. Wash your hands and arms thoroughly before eating or preparing food.
- Wear special work clothes and wash them separately from other laundry.
- If you are pregnant, avoid products containing lead, cadmium, or powdered pigments.
- If you have heart or kidney problems, check with your doctor before risking the high temperatures of foundry work.
- Be sure you have good ventilation: canopy hoods for furnaces and kilns, and specialized exhaust systems (vented outside) for welding.
- Use a respirator as a last resort. Be sure it is approved by the National Institute of Occupational Safety and Health (NIOSH) for the substance you are using.
- Wear protective equipment: welding helmet, goggles, face shield, safety shoes, hearing protectors, and fire resistant, asbestos-free work clothes and gloves.
- Never use solvents in welding areas.
- Substitute Sparex for other acids. Always add acid to water, not vice versa. Wear acid-proof gloves and goggles.
- Maintain machinery and inspect it regularly for electrical hazards. Keep long hair, clothing, and jewelry away from machinery and torches.
- When handling or storing fuel cylinders, remember:
  - to always double-check the contents of a new cylinder.
  - to move cylinders in an upright position with caps on.
  - to store cylinders securely, far from traffic, heat sources, and electric wires.
  - to use cylinders in the order they are received from the supplier.
  - when a cylinder runs out, close the valve and mark the cylinder as empty.
  - to store full and empty cylinders of each type of gas separately.
  - when you have finished working, close cylinder valves and put on valve protection caps. Release the pressure from regulators and hose lines before moving or storing the cylinders.

Photography

RISK FACTORS
• No North American data are available.

CONTRIBUTING FACTORS
• ingesting or inhaling chemicals
• chemical spills
• absorption of chemicals through skin
• poorly ventilated dark room
• failing to wear personal protection equipment

COMMENT

It is hard to imagine what the world would be like without photography. It is used in almost every activity that is of interest to people. Photography records events that make world history. It shows you faraway places and provides a record of your own family history.

Developing your own film is a rewarding part of photographic work, and many people have their own dark rooms and equipment. Whether you are experienced at developing photographs or just planning on taking it up as a hobby, there are some safety sense factors to consider with regard to the materials you will be using.

SAFETY SENSE

• Check into the specific health hazards of the materials you are using. Most products have a material data sheet that can be obtained from a craft guild or photography store. These data sheets provide valuable information on what is in the product and on how to handle it safely. Never work with a substance if you do not know what is in it.

• Read the manufacturers' directions of all substances carefully.
• If you are a novice, take a photography course; they are offered through most colleges and community recreation departments.
• Keep your work area clean. Chemicals can be just as dangerous when dry as they are in the liquid state. A powdery residue can be left on your counter or material, that can be

easily transferred into your body through your hands or lungs. Do a total clean-up of your dark room after every use.

- Wear protective equipment (eye goggles, rubber gloves, etc.) when handling chemicals and other dangerous substances.
- Label all chemicals clearly; put a date on them, since certain substances become contaminated and useless over time.
- Store all chemicals and other dangerous items in a locked, ventilated cabinet. If you have children or visiting grandchildren, keep your dark room locked when not using it.
- Ensure your dark room is ventilated to the outside with an exhaust fan of the appropriate size.

Printing and Graphic Arts

RISK FACTORS
- No North American data are available.

CONTRIBUTING FACTORS
- inhaling, absorbing, and ingesting acids, pigments, and solvents
- electrical shock and burns
- excessive noise

COMMENT

Printing and other graphic arts may not seem like the most dangerous hobbies in the world, but they do involve many of the same hazards as working in heavy industry. The best way to avoid accidents and injuries in this (or any) hobby is to know what the hazards are and how to steer clear of them.

The major dangers in printing and the graphic arts stem from the toxic chemicals and flammable materials used, the noise of the machinery, and electrical problems.

SAFETY SENSE

- Refer to a comprehensive reference work for the specific health hazards of materials you are using, or contact your local crafts guild. Never work with a material if you do not know what is in it.
- To keep down the level of dust and vapors in the air while you work, keep all containers closed except when you're using them.
- Clean spills with materials that readily absorb the liquid, such as paper towels or terry cloths.

- Follow manufacturers' recommendations for disposing of waste materials.
- Use gloves and barrier creams to protect your skin. Check that gloves are approved for the type of chemical you're handling.
- Wear a face mask and work in a well-ventilated area.
- Wear safety glasses when working with any material that could damage your eyes.

- Wash thoroughly after working with chemicals, paying close attention to cleaning your hands and fingernails.
- Never use solvents to clean any part of your body; they irritate the skin and can be absorbed into the bloodstream.
- Launder your work clothes often. Change your clothes immediately if you spill something on them.
- Never eat, drink, or smoke while working.
- Where possible, replace hazardous materials with safe ones -- ask for recommendations from your crafts guild.

Stained Glass

RISK FACTORS
- No North American data are available.

CONTRIBUTING FACTORS
- lead poisoning from inhaling lead fumes or dust, or from ingesting residual dust
- inhaling fumes from fluxes
- inadequate ventilation of the work area
- failing to wear protective equipment and clothing
- burns from equipment and chemicals
- improper handling of chemicals and materials
- fire
- flying particles of glass

COMMENT

Few things are more beautiful than art works in stained glass. Creating this beauty has its hazards, however -- the potential for lead poisoning is the major one. Fortunately, new lead-free solders have been produced and can be used for stained glass projects. They are not easy to use, but we strongly recommend them both for experienced crafts people and for beginners. Be aware, however, that some of these solders contain antimony, which is also toxic. You may want to try other ways that of binding the glass together, such as using channels of zinc.

SAFETY SENSE

- Avoid using lead.
- When using solder fluxes, such as zinc chloride, wear protective equipment; the residual from these fluxes can irritate your skin, eyes, and lungs. Fluoride fluxes are especially toxic -- avoid them altogether.
- Do not use asbestos board table tops, gloves, or other insulated materials containing asbestos.
- For metal coating the lead came and solder seams, the substances most often used are patinas, tinning solder fluxes, or copper that may be electroplated onto the seams. All these processes contain very toxic and caustic substances, such as fluorides, cyanide, and solvents.
- Plan studios and shops with health and safety in mind. If lead will be used, isolate the studio completely from living areas. Floors and surfaces should be made of materials that are easily sponged and mopped clean. Clean the work area frequently.
- Install ventilation systems appropriate for the work to be done. For example, provide local exhaust, such as slot vents or (if local codes permit)

a window exhaust fan at worktable level, for any operation that produces toxic emissions: soldering, tinning, dry cleaning (with whiting), polishing, applying patinas, etc.

- Provide local exhaust ventilation for dry grinding and polishing equipment. Remember, grinding lead glass can also expose you to lead and potential poisoning.
- Use wet methods whenever possible for grinding, polishing, and cutting. Clean wet grinding equipment when wet to avoid dust exposure. Clean water reservoirs often to remove scum.
- Equip grind wheels with face guards.
- Plan for fire safety. Install proper fire extinguishers, and post and practice fire evacuation procedures.
- Have electroplating done professionally, if possible. Otherwise, have safety experts help plan and design studio equipment, ventilation, and emergency facilities.
- Obtain material safety data sheets on all solders, abrasive grits and wheels, patinas, and other hazardous products. These sheets are available from any crafts guild.
- Avoid solders and other products containing significant amounts of arsenic, antimony, or other highly toxic metals.
- Keep children out of areas where lead or other toxic chemicals are used.
- Wear impact/dust goggles when cutting, grinding, or polishing glass.
- Keep a first-aid kit handy for cuts and accidents. Post emergency procedures. Use special "chain mail" types of safety gloves for especially hazardous procedures.
- Do not eat, smoke, or drink in the studio. Wash your hands after each work sessions.
- Wear protective clothing, such as a smock or coveralls, shoes, and hair covering. Wash work clothing often, separately from other clothes.
- Follow health, safety, and environmental protection regulations when you dispose of grinding and polishing dusts, spent or neutralized acids and other chemicals, waste glass, and other materials.
- Always be prepared to provide your doctor with precise information about the chemicals you use and your work practices. If you use lead, arrange for regular blood tests to monitor lead levels.

Woodworking

- No North American data are available.

CONTRIBUTING FACTORS
- inhaling wood dusts
- absorbing resins or glues through the skin
- lack of protective equipment and clothing
- fire
- poor ventilation of work areas
- allergic reactions to some woods
- noise
- machine vibration causing finger and hand numbness

COMMENT

Wood dusts, the most serious hazard in woodworking, are associated with a specific type of nasal and sinus cancer. Many wood dusts are toxic and can cause skin irritation, allergies, conjunctivitis, asthma, and serious lung damage. Rosewood, Canadian and western red cedar, cocobolo, mahogany, and satinwood are among the common offenders.

Particle board, plywood, preserved wood, and other composite forms are also hazardous, especially during sawing or sanding, because of the formaldehyde glues and resins they contain. Formaldehyde can cause allergic reactions, as well as irritation of the skin, eyes, and respiratory system. It is a suspected carcinogen.

Glues can be highly toxic and irritating when inhaled or brought into contact with skin. Among the most hazardous are formaldehyde-resin glues, which, when sanded after curing, may decompose into formaldehyde. Epoxy glues can cause allergic reactions and irritation to the skin, eyes, and respiratory system. Contact adhesives containing hexane are extremely flammable and can cause nerve damage. Those containing methylchloroform can, in large doses, contribute to heart problems.

SAFETY SENSE

- Learn from local crafts guilds about the hazards of the materials and processes you use.
- Avoid glues containing formaldehyde and solvents wherever possible.
- Ensure containers are well sealed when not in use.
- Never eat, drink, or smoke in the work area. Wash your hands and arms thoroughly before eating or preparing food.
- Wear eye protection and gloves.
- Wear special work clothes, and wash them separately from other laundry.
- Wet-mop or wet-vacuum all surfaces daily; sweeping stirs up dusts.
- Equip all dust-producing machinery with efficient dust collectors.
- Use a respirator when working with any material that produces large amounts of fine dust. Be sure it is approved by the National Institute for Occupational Safety and Health (NIOSH) for the particular substance you are using.
- Where there is minimum protection, always wear a dust mask.
- Ensure good exhaust ventilation wherever glues and solvents are used.
- When working with particle board and plywood, exhaust formaldehyde contaminated dusts to the outside.

PERSONAL PROTECTION

Industrial businesses are required by law to provide personal protection equipment for their employees, and most workers would never consider not wearing the safety boots, goggles, etc., that help them avoid injury on the job. Ironically, millions of these same employees will then go home in the family automobile not wearing a seat belt, and later play hockey at the local rink without a helmet.

Thousands of sports injuries could have been prevented, or the severity of the injury, minimized, if professional, amateur, and recreational athletes would use the protective equipment available to them.

Selecting the right equipment and being sure it fits properly, is the key to preventing many sports injuries. This is particularly true in direct contact or collision sports, such as football, hockey, and lacrosse, but it can also be true in non-contact sports and activities, such as bicycling, horseback riding, and soccer. Worry less about the color, look, and style of a piece of equipment and more about its ability to prevent injury. Try to explain the importance of this idea to your children.

Protective equipment should be certified by a recognized testing authority, such as the Canadian Standards Association (CSA), the American Society of Testing and Materials (ASTM), the Snell Memorial Foundation, or the American National Standards Institute (ANSI).

It is also important to properly maintain protective equipment, both to keep it in good repair and to determine when to throw it away. Too often old, worn out, ill-fitting equipment is passed down from one athlete to another (often from older child to younger child), compounding the risk of injury.

Keep the following principles in mind to make your sporting safer:

- **buy equipment from reputable manufacturers** (consult with your local sporting goods store);
- **buy the safest equipment possible** (a permanent disability will cost more than a good bicycle helmet);
- **make sure the equipment is assembled correctly** (follow the manufacturers' instructions to the letter);
- **maintain all equipment properly** (if the instructions say never to clean a helmet with a solvent -- don't);
- **use equipment only for the purpose for which it was designed** (metal cleats **do not** belong on a soccer field).

You may wish to have your protective equipment custom-made, especially if you compete at an advanced level. This will eliminate any problems with sizing, etc., that you may have with stock equipment carried in stores.

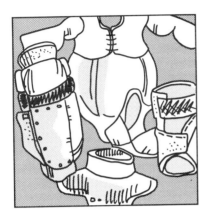

RISK FACTORS

- The body area (trunk, arms, legs, neck, and back) accounts for an estimated 53 percent of all sport-related injuries.

CONTRIBUTING FACTORS

- colliding with other players
- colliding with fixed objects
- exposure to heat or cold
- frostbite and hypothermia
- punctures
- falls

COMMENT

Body protection, for the shins, arms, chest, trunk, shoulders, and legs is essential in many contact and collision sports. This protection can include pads, girdles, bras, or even sun lotions.

SAFETY SENSE

- Shoulder pads must fit so that the neck opening allows the athlete to extend arms overhead without placing pressure on the neck. They must not, however, slide back and forth. Straps should hold the pads firmly, but not so firmly that they constrict soft tissue.
- Breast support is a must for women who participate in vigorous physical activity. Sport bras are available that provide the support needed. A bras should hold the breasts to the chest and prevent stretching of the Cooper's ligament.
- Thorax protection varies widely, from a mesh body suit with protective pads sewn into various areas to a

lightweight jacket with air-inflated pockets. Ask a sports physician about the type of protection needed for your sport.
- Hip and buttocks support is needed in collision sports, such as hockey, football, boxing, snow skiing, water skiing, and horseback riding. Commercial pads come in both girdle and belt types.
- Groin and genitalia protection is a must in some sports for both males and females.
- Limbs (arms, legs, ankles, and shins) are exposed to a great deal of injury in many sports. They require protection, and, where there is weakness, should be taped or supported with

an appropriate device. Don't neglect shins and lower legs -- there are many shin guards on the market. Knee supports and protective devices are abundant. The ones most commonly used are elastic knee, sleeves, pads, and braces.

- Ankle supports can be either an elastic or a spat type. The elastic type is a flexible, fibered sheath that slides over the foot and the ankle, giving mild support to a weak ankle.

The spat type is usually less resilient than elastic and has an open front. It fits directly over the ankle and ties snugly, like a shoe. Adhesive tape properly applied directly to the skin surface is probably the best method of providing protection.

- Many sports are played in conditions that increase the risk of skin problems, such as heat rashes caused by sweating. Refer any such problems to a physician immediately.

RISK FACTORS

- It is estimated that over 38,000 sport-related eye injuries are treated each year in hospital emergency rooms in North America. However, because many of the injured go directly to their doctors or are admitted directly into the hospital, the actual number of sport-related eye injuries may be two or more times greater than this estimate.
- For all age groups, eye injuries occur most frequently in baseball, hockey, basketball, racquet sports, and lacrosse.
- It is estimated that eye injuries account for four percent of all sport-related injuries.

CONTRIBUTING FACTORS

- hit by an object (stick, ball, puck)
- colliding with another player

COMMENT

While eye injuries in sports and recreational activities are relatively common, they are almost completely preventable. Loss of sight, even in one eye, involves a major change in lifestyle, and can have serious financial and social repercussions. It is, therefore, very important to reduce the risk of eye injury as much as possible by enforcing existing safety rules and, where necessary, by changing rules.

Coaches, physicians, and parents, should educate young athletes about the importance of eye protection in almost all sports.

The degree of protection needed depends on the risk associated with the activity. For example:

- Low-risk sports, such as track and field, swimming, and gymnastics, do not involve a thrown or hit ball, a bat or sticks, or close aggressive play (body contact).
- Sports with a moderate amount of risk, such as hockey, soccer, racquet sports (racquetball, squash, tennis, badminton, etc.), baseball, basketball, football, and volleyball, involve the use of a bat or stick, a high speed ball, close aggressive play (body contact), or a combination of these factors. Serious eye

injuries are common in these sports, but adequate eye protection devices are available.
- Combative sports, such as boxing, involve the greatest risk for eye injury. Effective eye protection devices have not yet been developed for these activities.

SAFETY SENSE

• Glass lenses, ordinary plastic lenses and open (lenseless) eye guards do **not** provide adequate protection.

• Moulded polycarbonate frames and lenses are suggested for persons who ordinarily wear contact lenses or no eyewear at all.

• Normal street-wear eyeglass frames with polycarbonate lenses 2 mm (0.08 in.) thick give adequate protection for routine use by active people. They are recommended for daily wear by visually-impaired or functionally one-eyed athletes. They are also satisfactory for athletes who wear eyeglasses in competition and who participate in low-risk sports.

• Select eye protectors certified by the Canadian Standards Association (CSA) or the American Society for Testing and Materials (ASTM).

• Follow the manufacturer's recommendations on maintenance and care of your eye protectors.

RISK FACTORS

- It is estimated that seven percent of all sport-related injuries affect the foot (including toes).

CONTRIBUTING FACTORS

- punctures
- poor playing surface
- improperly fitting foot protection
- poor-quality socks
- carelessness
- cuts
- crushing by an object
- scrapes
- sun or cold exposure

COMMENT

With the cost of top-of-the-line athletic shoes soaring, it is not unusual for an active family to invest hundreds of dollars a year in athletic shoes. There is now a special shoe for almost every sport, and some people who participate in several sports have one or more pairs of footwear for each sport.

Some may regard such an array of shoes as unnecessary, but your health and safety are two good reasons for purchasing the best possible shoe for each athletic activity. In most sports, the comfort and stability of the shoes worn affect performance and also can reduce the risk of injury.

The importance of shoes is most evident in such sports as running, race walking, basketball, volleyball, tennis, and other court sports that depend on a lot of foot activity. By wearing proper footwear, you can reduce the chances of developing syndromes, such as plantar fasciitis, shin splints, arch strain, blisters, and tendonitis.

In the safety sense tips below, we discuss only a few types of foot protection. Consult a sport athletic trainer, physician, coach, or sport store representative about shoes designed specifically for the activity you will be pursuing.

- Remember that, although shoe manufacturers now offer over 300 different size-width combinations, the correct length and width does not guarantee a good fit. If you have foot problems, consult a physician for advice.
- Buy footwear during the middle of the day. The size of your feet can increase about five percent just from walking on them.
- When buying sport footwear, always put on the type and number of socks that you will be wearing when participating in the activity.
- Wear clean socks, without holes, that are made of materials appropriate for the sport. Tube socks are not recommended because they do not have a heel to keep them in place on your foot. If two pair of socks are worn, a lightweight sock made of tightly woven material worn under a pair of heavy wool socks is the best combination. The lightweight sock prevents friction and the heavier sock drinks up moisture.
- Aerobic shoes must provide stability and shock attenuation in the front rather than the rear of the foot because your weight is usually on the lower part of the foot during aerobics. You may wish to consider shoes with support straps on the sides of the forefoot to increase stability.
- Tennis shoes should be heavier and more supportive than aerobic shoes to combat the stresses of sideways movement, as well as forward and backward running. The heel needs to be very rigid and the uppers are usually made of leather for additional structural support.
- Basketball shoes must be made of stiffer material than running shoes. The mid-sole should be firm and allow for shock absorption. High-top shoes give better ankle support. Leather tops are good, but should be perforated so perspiration can evaporate.
- Hiking boots should suit the type of terrain you will be walking over. They must provide good ankle support. Hiking boots are available with many types of soles, ranging from simple horizontal furrows to heavy cleats. The flexibility of the boot is important because it will result in less strain on the feet. Boots should be water resistant, breathable, and absorbent enough to draw perspiration away from the feet. Choose nylon laces, which will not rot, stretch, or break.

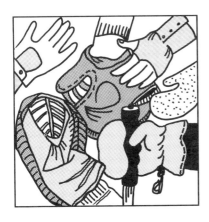

RISK FACTORS

- One study has reported that hand and wrist injuries account for 30 percent of all sport injuries in children, with boys having twice as many injuries as girls.
- It is estimated that injuries to the hand and wrist account for 20 percent of all sport-related injuries.
- Thumbs and fingers are the second most frequently injured parts of the body.

CONTRIBUTING FACTORS

- frostbite
- jamming the wrist, fingers, or hand into a solid object
- falls
- direct blow to the tip of a finger
- the finger, hand, or wrist getting hooked up in equipment
- burns
- overextending fingers or thumbs

COMMENT

When you consider how important our hands are to almost everything we do, it is amazing that the safety of the hand and wrist is often neglected in sports and recreational activities.

Special attention should be paid to protecting the hand not only from injury but from overuse. Constant stress to the hand can lead to irreversible damage, such as arthritis and permanent deformities later on in life.

SAFETY SENSE

- Protect your hands, fingers, and wrists from mechanical hazards, such as burns from ropes, machinery, and equipment.
- Never remove or tamper with the safety devices on sport and recreational vehicles, such as guards or kill switches.
- Remove watches, rings, and bracelets before engaging in a sport or other athletic activity.
- Protect your hands and wrists from irritating substances like chemicals, bacteria, fungi, and viruses. Barrier creams exist for this purpose.
- Wear hand and wrist protection whenever there is risk to them. There are many types available for various sports and recreational activities. You can also use tape to provide support for the hands, fingers, and wrists.

Head

RISK FACTORS
- Facial injuries (eye, head, cheek-bones, nose, etc.) account for an estimated 11 percent of all sports accidents.
- Head injuries account for about four percent of sport-related injuries.
- Eye injuries account for about four percent of all sport-related injuries.

CONTRIBUTING FACTORS
- hit by an object (a ball, stick, elbow, hand, etc.)
- colliding with other players
- colliding with fixed objects (fences, posts, trees, etc.)
- falls
- excessive noise

COMMENT

The governing bodies of most amateur sports regulate head protection for athletes. Each sport has its own requirements, depending upon the amount of body contact, missiles (balls, pucks, etc.), and the speeds involved. This protection may involve the use of helmets and face protectors.

Some athletes object to the use of such equipment, claiming that it obstructs vision or constrains movements. With modern equipment, however, these complaints are usually not valid. In fact, younger players who grow up with this equipment often say that they feel undressed if they play without the protection.

It has been proven that facial injuries can be nearly abolished, and the severity of injuries that do occur can be markedly decreased by the use of proper shields, helmets, mouthpieces, and ear guards.

Remember, even wearing a regular hat when walking, fishing, or jogging can provide protection against heat loss or heat stroke.

Helmets

- When selecting a helmet, be sure that it:
  - fits snugly;
  - covers the base of the skull;
  - does not come down over the eyes;
  - does not shift when manual pressure is applied;
  - does not recoil on impact;
  - has a chin strap that keeps the helmet from moving up and down or from side to side;
  - has provisions for attaching a face mask if required; and
  - is maintained according to manufacturer's instructions.

Face Guards

- Select a face guard that is:
  - light weight but strong;
  - non-irritating;
  - capable of withstanding frequent disinfecting; and
  - of the polycarbonate type (it should **not** contain corrosive metal).
- Be sure it is properly mounted.
- Check daily for defects.

Mouthgards

- Three basic types of mouthgards are available:
  - rigid, fixed-position, external shield or cage, attached to the helmet. This type of mouthguard offers good protection from frontal blows, but it must be positioned properly. Once attached to the helmet, it cannot be moved during play.
  - flexible, movable, worn externally, attached to the helmet. This type is currently the most popular among young hockey players, but does not provide adequate protection. It's inexpensive, but not recommended.
  - internal, fitted, plastic mouthguard. This type is worn inside the mouth and fits over the teeth, like mouth-

guards worn by boxers. It absorbs the shock of frontal blows and, when fitted properly, protects against blows from under the chin. There are two kinds of internal mouthguards:

a) custom made guards provide maximum protection. Have them fitted by a dentist or at a mouthguard clinic sponsored by local dental societies and/or health units. These mouthguards are recommended. Remember since they are custom fitted, they will need to be replaced periodically for growing children.

b) boilable mouthguards are sold at many sporting goods stores. This type can cause problems; you can fit them at home, but may not do it correctly. They're bulky and, during play, may cause difficulties for young people in speaking or breathing. This type is not recommended. Never fit one of these over braces or other oral appliances without consulting a dentist.

- Use an external and an internal mouthguard for maximum protection.
- Attach internal mouthguards securely to the faceguard of the helmet with a special tab.
- Never tamper with or pare down mouth protectors. Any alteration should be made by a dentist.

Ear Protection

- Wear ear protection when:
  - noise levels extend beyond 90 decibels. In some sports, for example, drag racing, and for using machines in recreational crafts, the noise levels could be very damaging even over a short time period.
  - outer ear damage is likely, such as in wrestling, boxing, martial arts, etc.

SPECIALTY TOPICS

Alcohol

Alcohol is a contributing factor in many sports and recreational injuries. For example, 42 percent of all boating accident victims had been drinking alcohol. Alcohol is also involved in approximately 40 percent of all motor vehicle deaths. Many of these deaths occur while travelling to and from recreational activities, such as camping trips, visits to the cottage, and sporting events.

Many people do not realize that even a few drinks before, during, or after a game can impair their judgment enough to cause injuries. Even as a spectator at a sporting event you can fall down the stairs or get in a traffic accident. Use alcohol responsibly.

Your tolerance for alcohol and the amount of food in your stomach influence your state of impairment. However, the most important factor is the concentration of alcohol in your blood. The following chart will assist you in estimating this concentration.

1. Count your drinks [one drink equals 43 ml (1½ oz.) of spirits or 85 ml (3 oz.) of wine or 341 ml (12 oz.) of beer].

2. Refer to the chart on the next page. Under the number of drinks and opposite your body weight, find the percent of blood alcohol listed.

3. It takes the body about one hour to eliminate one drink [e.g., 43 ml (1½ oz.) of spirits], so subtract the percent of alcohol burned up in your body during the time elapsed since your first drink. The resulting number would represent approximately your present blood alcohol concentration. Remember, this is only an estimate. Other factors, such as experience in drinking, amount of food in your stomach, etc., will affect your state of impairment. Remember that .10% equals 100 mg% or .08% equals 80 mg%.

| BODY | NUMBER OF DRINKS IN MG % | | | | | | | | |
WEIGHT	1	2	3	4	5	6	7	8	9
45KG (100 LBS)	43	87	130	174	217	261	304	348	319
56KG (125 LBS)	34	69	103	139	173	209	242	278	312
68KG (150 LBS)	29	58	87	116	145	174	203	232	261
79KG (175 LBS)	25	50	75	100	125	150	175	200	225
90KG (200 LBS)	22	43	65	87	108	130	152	174	195
102KG (225 LBS)	19	39	58	78	97	117	136	156	175
113KG (250 LBS)	17	37	52	70	87	105	122	139	156
Hours since drinking started		1		2		3		4	
% of alcohol burned		15mg%		30mg%		45mg%		60mg%	

Example: Based on the chart, a 56 kg (125 lb) person who consumes three drinks in one hour has an approximate blood alcohol level of 103 mg%. After a two-hour time lapse, his blood alcohol level is 73 mg% (103-30=73).

Athletes With Disabilities

The number of athletes with disabilities participating in competitive sports is rapidly increasing. Wheelchair sports have evolved from rehabilitation exercises to serious competition on the local, state/provincial, national, and international levels. Wheelchair athletes have now broken the four-minute mile barrier and can finish a marathon in less than two hours. Visually and hearing impaired athletes compete on the same level as other athletes in competitive activities, such as swimming, wrestling, and running. As the number of participants and the level of competition increases, so will the frequency of injuries sustained by athletes with disabilities.

Like other athletes, athletes with disabilities are prone to strains, sprains, lacerations, abrasions, and other injuries. Because athletes with disabilities can and do participate in all kinds of sport and recreational activities, the following safety sense advice covers the general precautions for these athletes. Athletes with disabilities are to refer to the section on the sport or recreational activity in which they participate for additional safety sense tips.

Athletes with disabilities are cautioned to ensure that they receive instructions from a competent trainer or coach, since each sport has its own particular hazards and equipment needs.

SAFETY SENSE

- To prevent being injured by motor vehicles, wheelchair distance runners, etc., should train on a track and not on public roads.
- Overuse injuries occur among athletes. Frequent rest breaks during training must be scheduled.
- As with all sport and recreational activities, competition can become very physical. Pushing, bumping, and falling out of wheelchairs, for example, can cause injuries. Obeying game rules, good coaching, and competent refereeing will reduce these injuries.
- All injured athletes must rest and care properly for injuries before resuming play.
- Athletes should use a weight training program to develop their muscles.
- The facility area used for activities should be large enough for every-

one to practice and play without crowding.

- The facility area should have sufficient hazard-free boundary space surrounding the activity.
- Hazards that cannot be removed should be clearly marked and padded against impact.
- Activity areas should be accessible to all participants.
- Participants must be given a thorough orientation to the facility, such as distance between the pool entrance, the deck, and the pool.
- Equipment should vary in size and be modified, if necessary, for the athlete with a disability.
- Sports equipment must be appropriate to the sport.
- Instructions must be provided so that everyone can understand, see, and hear the demonstrations.
- Capable assistance must be provided when needed on an individual basis.
- Instructors must be trained in emergency first-aid.
- Instructional content must be designed for the developmental and skill level of the athlete.
- Instructional content must be taught in a generally progressive order of difficulty, with safety procedures a part of each step.
- All athletes must participate in a physical conditioning program designed for the specific sport in which they are participating.
- Heat-related problems, such as exhaustion and cramps, must be closely supervised by officials, coaches, and trainers.

Children and Youth

Millions of children and youth participate in recreational activities, organized youth leagues, and interscholastic sports programs. Although they enjoy and benefit from these activities, between three and 11 percent of participants are injured in sports programs each year. Football, basketball, gym games, baseball, and roller-skating have the highest injury rates. Studies have also shown that unorganized activities account for many injuries. The following safety sense tips can minimize injury among children and youth.

SAFETY SENSE

- Proper conditioning before and during the competitive season builds muscle strength, muscle endurance, aerobic endurance, flexibility, and acclimatization to heat.
- Excessive training, training for multiple sports, and sudden changes in training practices may put excessive stress on the athlete's musculoskeletal system.
- Optimal maintenance of the recreational area may reduce the risk of injury from falls. For example, the careful maintenance of ski slopes and football fields reduces injury rates.
- Athletes who have sustained injuries in the past are more likely to injure themselves again. To reduce the risk of reinjury:
  - ensure that the injury heals completely;
  - provide the appropriate rehabilitation;

- restore conditioning and skill level before resuming competition; and
- provide external bracing support.
- Young athletes require close supervision by coaches and medical personnel to ensure that they receive appropriate conditioning and practice safe techniques. For example, supervisors on the ski slope, spotters in the gymnasium, and medical personnel on the soccer field will help reduce injury rates.
- Modified rules can help reduce injuries in some sports. For example, do not allow bodychecking in hockey.
- Instruct athletes on the proper techniques and skills for their activity. For example, using a poor pitching technique in baseball can cause elbow problems.
- Safety equipment reduces the risk of injury. Make sure that well-maintained equipment of the

appropriate size is available to participants.

- Athletes should have medical examinations on a regular basis. Physicians should be informed about the activities in which the youth participate so they can watch for specific problems.

- Competitors in collision sports should be well-matched according to weight, age, and/or skill level to ensure fair and safe play.

Drugs

Do you know someone who is dying to win? You might, if you know an athlete who is taking drugs to improve her or his performance or physique. Drugs can be very harmful if not properly prescribed by a doctor for a genuine medical condition. Many of the drugs banned in sport can harm an athlete's health. In addition, taking drugs constitutes cheating. In this section, we discuss the misuse of drugs to improve performance in sports.

SAFETY SENSE

- Don't drink alcohol. Although alcohol may improve psychological functioning, it consistently impairs psychomotor performance and information processing. Even small amounts of alcohol impair reaction time, hand and eye coordination, accuracy, balance, and gross motor skills. Problems in any of these areas can lead to an accident.
- Don't use stimulants. An overdose can cause death. Side effects include high blood pressure, strokes, and the inability to recognize that you have received a serious injury. Over a prolonged period of time, addiction is also a major concern.
- Don't use narcotic analgesics, such as morphine, heroin, or codeine. These drugs are banned because they hide the effects of illness and injury and can lead to addiction, exhaustion, overtraining, constipation, apathy, and death.
- Don't use anabolic steroids. In men, prolonged abuse can cause shrinking and hardening of the testicles. In women, it can cause the development of "male-type" physical characteristics. It can cause liver cancer in either sex. Steroid use is especially dangerous for children -- it can stunt their growth.
- Don't use corticosteroids. Overdoses or prolonged use can cause high blood pressure, salt and water retention, potassium loss, and bone and muscle weakness. Diabetes is another possible complication. Like anabolic steroids, corticosteroids can stunt the growth of children.

Elderly Athletes

It is very difficult to define an elderly athlete. The criterion can be chronological years, physical ability, etc. If you personally consider yourself to be an elderly athlete, you may wish to consider the following safety sense tips to avoid injury.

SAFETY SENSE

- Make sure you warm up for 20 to 25 minutes before a workout. Stretching increases blood circulation and muscle temperature, making you more flexible and decreasing the chance of muscle strain. Rotating your joints counteracts their stiffness.
- Don't overdo it. Most injuries happen in the first 15 minutes when muscles are not warmed up, or in the last 15 minutes of a game when players are overtired.
- Make sure you cool down. This prevents the blood from pooling in your muscles and making you faint. When your workout is over, blood is still racing through your body and it piles up in the muscles, robbing circulation to the brain. Stretching after a workout sends blood back through your heart to your brain.
- Don't switch suddenly between physical activities. Interestingly, many athletes pull muscles doing odd jobs around the house. Some athletes don't realize that their muscles aren't properly toned for all sports. A good downhill skier might have strong leg muscles, but lack the upper body strength to chop wood without causing injury. If you switch to a sport requiring use of different muscle groups, follow a specific exercise program, perhaps including light weightlifting, one month in advance.
- Cool your desire to win. Too often, elderly athletes don't recognize that overexertion and recklessness can lead to injuries.
- See a physician who is knowledgeable about sports injuries.
- Take precautions to protect your knee joints, ankles, elbows, shoulders, and lower back from wear and tear. Runners with sore knee joints should try running on softer surfaces. Tennis players should switch to clay or grass courts and only take part in doubles games. If the pain continues, switch to less demanding sports. Try cycling or swimming.
- Treat your injuries immediately.

Fair Play

How often have you finished a game feeling that you were cheated by your competitors? Have you ever thought a game wasn't fun because your parents or coach were mad that you didn't win? Fair play in its broadest sense means enjoying a sport or recreational activity. It doesn't mean violence, winning at all costs, or poor sportsmanship. It involves fun, friendly competition, and individual satisfaction. Hopefully, following these safety sense tips will contribute to fair play in your recreational activities.

SAFETY SENSE

- Play for enjoyment.
- Obey the rules.
- Control your emotions.
- Be a good sport.
- Treat all players with respect.
- Be a team player: cooperate and share.
- If you are a coach or parent:
  - be generous with your praise;
  - ensure that all participants follow the rules;
  - provide a safe environment to play in;
  - use all players -- don't show favoritism;
  - don't set unattainable standards;
  - don't take winning more seriously than everything else;
  - support the volunteer referees, don't harass them; and
  - teach the long-term benefits of recreational activity such as physical fitness.
- If you are a spectator:
  - show respect for coaches, referees, and players;
  - respect the referee's decisions; and
  - applaud both teams.

Flash Floods

Campers in North America's wilderness areas should be prepared to face certain dangers. Maps, first-aid kits, proper clothing, and equipment are all part of the experienced camper's gear. A knowledge of natural hazards, such as dangerous animals and toxic plants, is also important. But one danger that the unwary camper may learn of only after it's too late is the flash flood -- a potential killer. Flash floods can occur after heavy rain under conditions in which water runs off very rapidly from areas of higher elevation to low-lying areas, causing the natural drainage system to overflow with rushing water, rocks, mud, uprooted trees, and other debris.

SAFETY SENSE

- Stay away from natural stream beds, arroyos, and other drainage channels during and after rainstorms.
- Use your maps. Know when you are on relatively low ground. You don't have to be at the bottom of a hill to be in danger of flash floods.
- Know where high ground is and how to get there in a hurry. Remember, many roads and trails run parallel to drainage patterns and may be swept away by flood water.
- Stay out of flooded areas; the water may still be rising and the current is usually swift. Never try to cross a flowing stream on foot if the water is above your knees.
- Abandon stalled vehicles if you can do so safely. Flood waters may rise and sweep away the vehicle (and its occupants). Attempts to move stalled vehicles from a flooded area have resulted in many deaths.
- Keep alert to signs of rain nearby or in distant hills, especially at night. A flash flood can catch you while you sleep.
- Stay tuned to local radio or television stations for information on developing weather and flood conditions.
- If you are out of the range of broadcast information, be sure to watch for indicators of flash flooding. These include an increased speed of river flow and a rise in river level. Be prepared to move to safety.
- Many community developments use storm drainage ponds. These large underground excavations store water temporarily during heavy rains, then release it slowly into the regular storm sewer system to prevent flooding. Because these drainage ponds generally grassed over, they are great play areas for the residents. However, you should leave the area immediately when heavy rain is forecast; when these ponds are full, you can drown in them.

Getting Lost

Emergency and rescue teams respond to approximately 700 calls each year in North America. One study found that two-thirds of lost people are between the ages of 10 and 19.

You don't have to be wandering in trackless back country to get lost. A wilderness emergency can happen just about anywhere a person suddenly loses those things she or he relies upon for direction, e.g. land marks.

Search and rescue experts have described the typical feelings and reactions of lost people. Even familiar places may look strange. They will feel compelled to press on, to hurry and find "the right place." As their sense of helplessness grows, they may race around frantically -- and uselessly -- discarding equipment and even clothing. They may lose their sense of time completely. Panic often prevents them from responding to searchers or may even cause them to hide from them.

Children are especially vulnerable. They may not respond because they are afraid of strangers or afraid they will be punished for causing trouble. They may interpret the searchers' shouting as anger. Searchers draped with ropes, carrying blaring walkie-talkies, and headlamps, tramping around in the dark, may even appear as monsters. Teaching your children now to respond to searchers can increase their chances of being among the 96 percent of lost people found alive.

SAFETY SENSE

- Before setting out on a hiking or camping trip, prepare a basic survival kit for each person, even children. The kit should include the following:
  - **a pocketknife and waterproof matches** for those old enough to use them safely;
  - **a plastic trash bag, preferably brightly colored**, to wear as a poncho stuffed with leaves, grass, or pine needles to protect against the cold;
  - **A whistle on a string around your neck** -- you can blow a whistle longer and louder than you can shout -- and the sound may travel farther;
  - **a metal or plastic mirror** -- sun flashes off a mirror can be seen as far as 32 km (20 mi.) away; and

- **high energy food and a canteen of water**. Few searches last longer than two or three days, so starving is unlikely. But some food -- a handful of hard candy and some complex carbohydrates, such as granola bars -- will help keep up your morale as well as your energy.
• If you get lost, don't wander. Searchers will begin looking for you where you were last seen.
• Think and rest to prevent yourself from panicking. Sit down, drink some water, and eat some food. Then ask yourself who will notice you are missing and when they will become concerned. Imagine what that person will do and consider how you can best respond.
• Plan. Empty your pockets and your pack, and think about how you can use what you find to help yourself. Sometimes people have all the equipment they need to survive, but forget to use it.
• Orient yourself to your surroundings and activate your survival attitude. Your best survival tool is your brain.

Hypothermia

It is difficult to determine how many of the estimated 5,500 people who drown annually in North America die because of hypothermia -- losing body heat faster than they can produce it. The major areas of heat loss include the head, chest, and groin area. Excessive exposure to cold can lead to exhaustion, shivering, slurred speech, loss of memory, disorientation, irregular pulse, loss of consciousness, and, finally, cardiac arrest.

SAFETY SENSE

- If you fall into cold water (below 21° C/70° F) and cannot get out immediately, a life jacket or personal flotation device will help keep you afloat. It will also help decrease the amount of energy you expend and to insulate your body against heat loss.
- Never leave a boat unless absolutely necessary. Get back in, climb on top, or hold on. Do not attempt to swim to shore. Swimming uses up energy and heat.
- Keep your clothes on.
- Adopt a tuck position -- cross your ankles, cross your arms over your chest, lean back, and try to relax. This position reduces body heat loss by up to 50 percent. If you are with a group of people, you should all huddle together.
- Cold temperatures on land can also produce hypothermia. If you become stranded in the cold, shelter yourself from the wind and rain. Replace wet clothes with dry warm clothes or blankets, and move around to increase body heat. Drink hot, high-energy liquids, such as sugared tea and hot chocolate. Finally, it is very important to stay awake.

Play Areas

Children all over the world play -- in backyards, in parks, on school grounds, or wherever else they happen to be. Play is the major recreational activity of children. Many accidents happen during play, and most of them are hard to prevent. However, five factors can minimize injuries without totally eliminating fun: proper selection of play equipment, safe surfaces under the equipment, thorough maintenance of equipment, plenty of supervision, and training children in safety sense.

SAFETY SENSE

- Some knowledge of child development is important for choosing and designing play areas. The type of equipment, its size, and its degree of challenge should be appropriate for the age groups of the children who will use it. Information on proper equipment is usually available at public libraries and community recreation departments.
- Because 60 to 70 percent of children who fall from playground equipment land on the ground, it is important to provide a soft landing surface, especially where young children will play. Sand is the best choice, and grass is better than concrete.
- Any play equipment is potentially dangerous if not properly maintained. Concrete footings for fixed equipment must be set deep enough to avoid their working

through to the surface of the ground. Sand boxes should not be covered since rain and sun purify sand; if necessary, they can be protected from animals by wire netting. Wooden equipment should have rounded edges and very smooth surfaces to prevent splinters.
- Children can hurt themselves on even the best equipment if they are not properly supervised. Swimming pools should be completely off limits when adults are not around. The degree of supervision necessary depends upon the age and maturity of the children. Parents should also enforce rules about where children can play; having the safest backyard in town will not help if your children spend their time playing by the railway tracks.

- Children should learn where it is safe to play, how to use their equipment properly, and what stunts they should not try. By teaching children to play responsibly and to call for help when they need it, you encourage them to learn caution and common sense in all areas of their lives.

Pregnancy and Recreational Activities

Current thinking is that moderate physical activity during pregnancy is beneficial. An expectant mother who exercises generally feels more energetic and is better able to cope with the physical strains of pregnancy.

SAFETY SENSE

- Consult your doctor at the beginning of your pregnancy to discuss the types of exercises and activities in which you wish to participate.
- Never begin a strenuous exercise program during pregnancy if you were previously doing little or no exercise.
- Avoid dehydration and overheating. Raising your core temperature above 38.5° C (101° F) may cause growth deformities in the fetus. Never exercise in hot, humid weather and never use hot tubs or whirlpools.
- Do not let your heart rate exceed 140 beats per minute during exercise.
- Avoid sharp, jerky movements.
- After 18 weeks of pregnancy, do not exercise while lying on your back. This position could interrupt the return of blood to your heart. If you feel light-headed or faint, quickly roll over to your side.
- Do not exercise if you have any bleeding or spotting.
- Stop exercising until you talk to your doctor if you experience dizziness or pain in your back, joints, head, or chest.
- Don't exercise if you have a virus. A virus will put enough strain on your body.
- Always start any physical activity with a complete, gradual warm up and end with a cool down.
- Wear a good sports bra or support bra during exercise to prevent breast injury.

Rings and Other Jewelry in Sports

Many athletes are not aware of the dangers of wearing rings and other jewelry during sports and recreational activities. These dangers are well known in industry, where many occupations have safety programs that forbid the wearing of some jewelry. However, they are not sufficiently emphasized in sports and recreational activities, except boxing, football, and wrestling, where hand and facial injuries are common.

SAFETY SENSE

- Remove all rings and jewelry before participating in a sport or recreational activity.
- Seek emergency medical treatment immediately for ring-related injuries to your fingers. Attempts to save a damaged finger are often unsuccessful because skin, nerves, vessels, tendons, and even bones and joints are damaged. Even if you do not lose the finger, it may not work very well.
- Although rings are especially dangerous, other jewelry can also lead to injury. For example, a necklace can bounce up and hit your eye or distract you from the task at hand.

Saunas, Whirlpools, and Hot Tubs

For some people, reclining in a sauna, whirlpool, or hot tub is the height of relaxation -- but it is not without hazards. Intense heat, water, and electricity are all involved. The danger increases whenever alcohol is involved. Alcohol, a relaxant-depressant, dilates your capillaries, reddening your skin and creating a feeling of general relaxation. Since heat produces the same results, the combination may be overwhelming. Remember this when you are next tempted to soak in a hot tub with a glass of wine.

SAFETY SENSE

- If you suffer from heart disease, diabetes, high blood pressure, or low blood pressure, do not enter a sauna, whirlpool, or hot tub without consulting your doctor first.
- Always check the water temperature before getting in. Never allow the temperature of a whirlpool or hot tub to exceed 40° C (104° F).
- Never use a sauna, whirlpool, or hot tub while under the influence of alcohol, anticoagulants, antihistamines, vasoconstrictors, vasodilators, stimulants, hypnotics, narcotics, or tranquilizers.
- Staying in a sauna, whirlpool, or hot tub only for a short time; long exposure may result in nausea, dizziness, or fainting. If you wish, return for another brief stay after showering and cooling down.
- Always enter and exit slowly and cautiously.
- Never allow children to use a sauna, whirlpool, or hot tub without supervision. Keep the equipment locked or covered to prevent them from playing in it.
- Avoid using a sauna, whirlpool, or hot tub alone.
- List the following emergency numbers by the nearest phone: police, fire and/or rescue unit, physician, ambulance, and hospital.
- Shower before and after a sauna, hot tub, or whirlpool session. Wear a bathing cap to protect yourself against scalp infections such as ringworms.
- Keep your sauna, hot tub, and whirlpool clean to prevent the breeding

and transmittal of bacteria, such as diarrhea, vaginitis, and athlete's foot.

- Make sure all electrical plugs have a ground fault interrupter to protect you against electrical shocks.
- Use non-skid flooring around the equipment to help prevent slips and falls.
- Keep electrical appliances, such as radios, stereos, and bar fridges, out of the area.

- Set the timer switch on the equipment to the manufacturer's recommended limit for exposure. Install the switch well out of the reach of children.
- Avoid using a sauna, whirlpool, or hot tub if you are pregnant. A pregnant woman's large circulatory system can transmit excessive heat to an unborn child.

Signalling for Help

Maybe you will need to signal for help only once in your life. Your ultralight plane may need to land in an emergency situation; you could be stranded outdoors with an all-terrain vehicle or motorcycle; a motor failure on your boat could leave you stranded; or you may be lost in the woods. Whatever the reason, once is enough that you should know how to signal for help correctly and be prepared to do so.

SAFETY SENSE

- A well-known distress signal is flying the national flag upside down.
- An internationally recognized distress signal flag is a fluorescent orange-red cloth 114 to 182 cm (45 to 72 in.), on which there is a 45 cm (18 in.) diameter black circle and a 45 cm (18 in.) black square. All boaters, pilots of light planes, and people venturing into wilderness areas should carry this flag.
- Many boating supply, sporting, and aircraft supply stores sell shatterproof survival signal mirrors. They are mirrored on one side, painted black on the other, and have a hole in the middle so it can be aimed to reflect sunlight. These shafts of light are visible up to 32 km (20 mi.) away.
- Red-orange smoke is an internationally recognized distress signal.

Bombs that emit this smoke for about five minutes can be bought in boating supply stores.
- Red pyrotechnic flares are useful in a wide range of emergency situations, from road accidents to boat accidents. They are also useful for signalling passing aircraft. Handle them with care as they can start fires.
- You can use ordinary flashlights as distress signals by flashing SOS -- three short flashes, three long flashes, then three short flashes. Pause, then begin again.
- A powerful distress signal is a flare gun that can fire flares to very high altitudes. Buy these in a boating or aircraft supply store.
- Emergency locator radios are very efficient emergency signalling devices, especially now that satellites

can pinpoint their locations. These radios are readily available.

- If you do not have a signalling device, try to mark out a message, a cross, or SOS. Tramp them in snow, or mark them out with bushes and boughs. In a real emergency, you can set fires in the shape of SOS or at the corners of a triangle. However, take care not to start an uncontrolled fire.
- Other simple distress signals are: waving your arms, waving a shirt overhead, blowing a whistle or horn, and raising one oar upright in a boat.

Sportsmanship

Too often, injuries occur because participants have violated the rules or lost their tempers. Athletes are often pushed by coaches and parents to win at all costs. Some sports and recreational leagues are so competitive that the comraderie and fun are lost. In order to promote sportsmanship in its truest sense, follow these tips.

SAFETY SENSE

- Coaches and parents should act in the best interest of the athlete's development as a whole person.
- Coaches and participants must recognize that many rules are necessary to protect athletes from injury. Officials should interpret and apply these rules fairly and forcefully.
- Coaches must show athletes and other participants courtesy, good faith, and respect.
- Coaches and athletes should display the highest standard of personal conduct, both on and off the playing area.
- Spectators should not interfere with the athletes, officials, coaches, or the activity itself.

Sun and Heat

To prevent the problems associated with physical activity in the heat, you must know what they are. (1) **Heat rash** is an inflammation of the skin that causes irritation. (2) **Heat cramps** occur when an excessive amount of body fluid is lost through sweating and the body is low on minerals, such as sodium and potassium. (3) **Heat fainting** is caused by changes in blood distribution, the pooling of blood in the legs, or the increased need for blood flow in the skin to cool the body. (4) **Heat exhaustion** occurs when the circulatory and thermoregulatory systems cannot keep pace with the demands the athlete is making on his or her body. This condition is especially serious and may be fatal in older individuals and people with heart problems. (5) **Heat stroke** is the eventual result of heat exhaustion. It is a life-threatening condition that requires immediate treatment by medical professionals.

SAFETY SENSE

- If you get a **heat rash**, simply avoid the heat for a few days.
- If you get a **heat cramp**, relax mentally and physically. Replace lost minerals in your body by drinking a teaspoon of salt dissolved in a glass of water. If you suffer another heat cramp within 30 minutes, you should rest for the day.
- Sufferers of **heat fainting** should be laid down in a cool place with their feet elevated.
- People who are overcome with **heat exhaustion** must quit all activity. They should cool themselves immediately using any means available, including rubbing themselves with ice, drinking cold liquids, and removing their clothing.

- **Heat stroke** victims must be transported to a hospital and cooled immediately by whatever means possible.
- Hold practice sessions in the early morning and the evening when it is less hot and humid.
- Always have plenty of fluids available.
- In very physically demanding activities, let your body gradually become accustomed to the heat. Generally, you will need a two-week period of reduced exposure for your body to adjust to hot weather.
- You are more vulnerable to the heat if:
  - you are unaccustomed to playing in the heat;

- you are overweight;
- you overexert yourself, especially before you are properly conditioned; or
- you have an infection, fever, or gastrointestinal disturbance.
• Wear light-weight clothing that is loose-fitting at the neck, waist, and sleeves.
• Wear clean clothing -- it will breathe more easily.
• Take rest breaks often in very hot, humid conditions.

REFERENCE ORGANIZATIONS

American Society Testing and Materials
Art Hazards Information Center, New York
Biathlon Ski
Canada Safety Council
Canadian Amateur Bobsled and Luge Association
Canadian Amateur Boxing Association
Canadian Amateur Diving Association
Canadian Amateur Football Association
Canadian Amateur Hockey Association
Canadian Amateur Rowing Association
Canadian Amateur Softball Association
Canadian Amateur Speed Skating Association
Canadian Amateur Swimming Association
Canadian Amateur Wrestling Association
Canadian Badminton Association
Canadian Blind Sports Association Inc.
Canadian Canoe Association
Canadian Centre for Occupational Health and Safety
Canadian Coast Guard
Canadian Colleges Athletic Association
Canadian Cycling Association
Canadian Equestrian Federation
Canadian Federation of Amateur Baseball
Canadian Federation of Sport Organizations for the Disabled
Canadian Fencing Association
Canadian Field Hockey Association
Canadian Gymnastics Federation
Canadian Lacrosse Association
Canadian Ladies' Golf Association
Canadian Orienteering Federation
Canadian Racquetball Association
Canadian Rhythmic Sportive Gymnastics Federation
Canadian Rugby Association
Canadian Ski Association
Canadian Soccer Association
Canadian Sport Parachuting Association
Canadian Squash Racquets Association
Canadian Standards Association
Canadian Table Tennis Association
Canadian Team Handball Federation
Canadian Track and Field Association
Canadian Volleyball Association
Canadian Water Polo Association
Canadian Water Ski Association
Canadian Weightlifting Federation
Canadian Wheelchair Sports Association

REFERENCE ORGANIZATIONS CONT'D

Canadian Yachting Association
Consumer and Corporate Affairs Canada, Canadian Electronic
  Injury Surveillance System (CEISS)
Cross Country Ski
Curl Canada
Emergency Preparedness Canada
Federation of Canadian Archers Inc.
Federation of Deaf Sports of Canada
Health and Welfare Canada
Judo Canada
Ministry of Tourism and Recreation, Ontario
National Electronic Injury Surveillance System (NEISS)
National Karate Association
National Safety Council, USA
Nordic Combined Ski Discipline
Régie de la sécurité dans les sports du Québec, Québec
Ringette Canada
Royal Canadian Golf Association
Shooting Federation of Canada
Ski Jumping Discipline
Sport Information Resource Centre, Canada
Sport Medicine Council of Canada
Synchro Canada
U.S. Consumer Product Safety Commission

ABOUT THE AUTHOR

Heward Grafftey received his bachelor of arts degree at Mount Allison University, majoring in political science and history, and his bachelor of civil law degree at McGill University before being admitted to the bar of the province of Québec.

Before entering Parliament, he was Chairman and Chief Executive Officer of the Montreal Lumber Company Limited. He was the federal Member of Parliament for the Québec riding of Brome-Missisquoi from 1958-68 and 1972-80. In 1962, Grafftey was named Parliamentary Secretary to the Minister of Finance, and was a delegate to the United Nations in 1958 and 1966. In 1979, he became the Minister of State for Social Programs and Minister for Science and Technology in the Clark administration.

During his parliamentary career, Grafftey co-authored an all-party brief on motor vehicle and highway deaths and injuries, and appeared before the Senate and the House of Representatives of the United States Congress, as well as various state legislatures on the subject. He has been an advocate for government-sponsored research into the development of a prototype safety car. He has also played an active role in improving community emergency response systems. Grafftey has written many articles on accident prevention. He is also author of the books The Senseless Sacrifice: A Black Paper on Medicine, Lessons from the Past, Trust the People: How Canadians Get Governments and Leaders They Don't Want, Safety Sense on the Road, and Safety Sense in the Home.

He was named Queen's Counsel in 1981. He currently resides in Ottawa, where he has a practice in government relations with emphasis in the area of technological innovation. Mr. Grafftey is the Chairman of Safety Sense Enterprises.

233

NOTES